THIS IS MY STORY

& MY SONG

Gospel Favorites
for
Piano and Organ

Arranged by PAUL FERRIN

ORGAN – MODERATE   PIANO – MODERATELY ADVANCED

PUBLISHING COMPANY

Lillenas.com

CONTENTS

Blessed Assurance 3

Come and Dine 29

How Great Our Joy!
    with **Angels from the Realms of Glory** 73

Like a River 60
    Like a River Glorious
    Peace Like a River

Nearer, Still Nearer 38

O the Deep, Deep Love of Jesus 86

Turn Your Eyes upon Jesus 51

Wonderful Grace of Jesus 16

Blessed Assurance

Sw. Flutes 8' 4' 2', Principal 4'
Gt. Principal 8', Flutes 8' 4' 2', Octave 4', Sw. to Gt.
Ped. Principal 16', Bourdon 16', Octave 8', Flute 8'

PHOEBE PALMER KNAPP
Arranged by Paul Ferrin

start slowly and accel.

Freely, with feeling

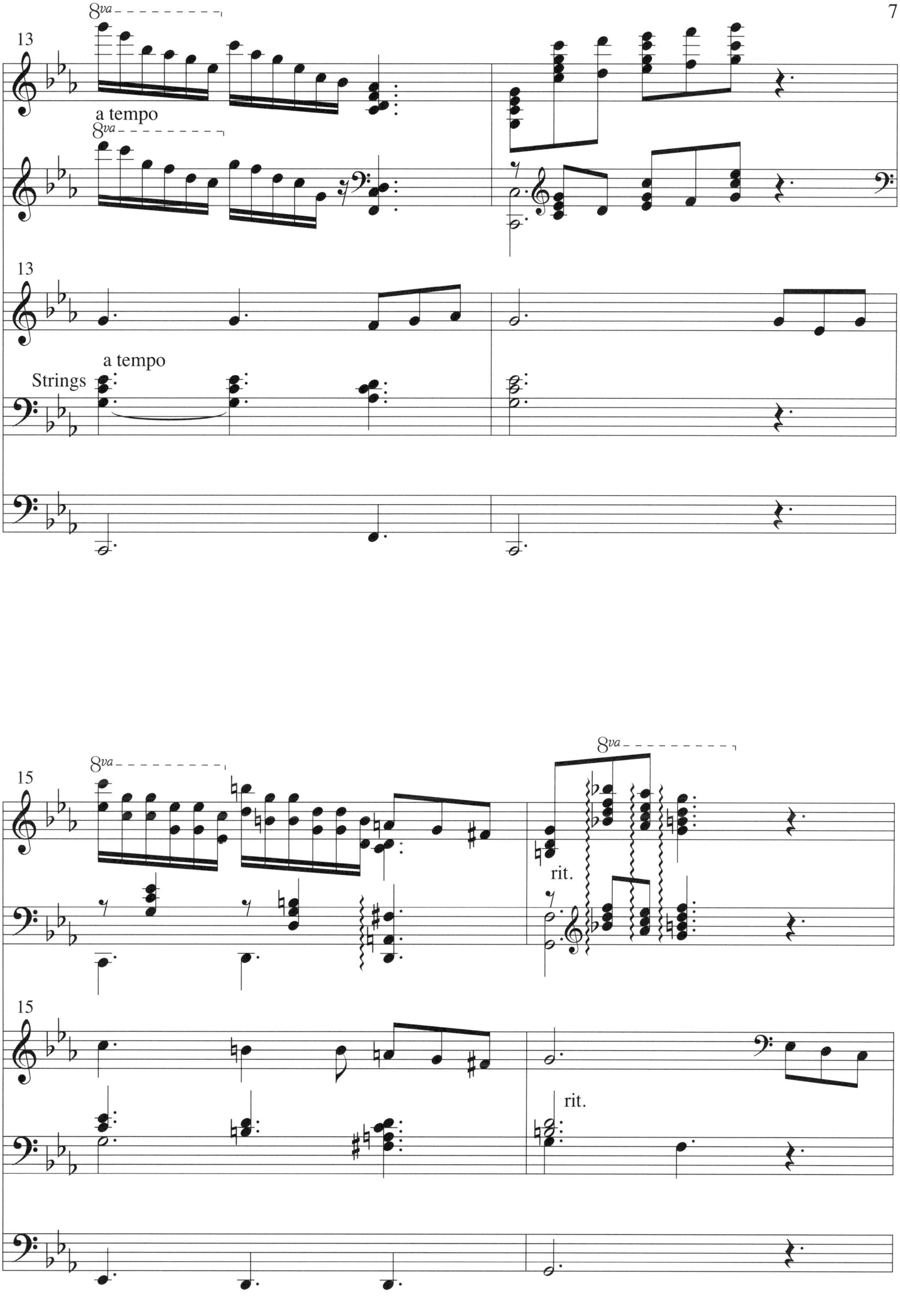
13
8va
a tempo
8va
13
a tempo
Strings
15
8va
8va
rit.
15
rit.

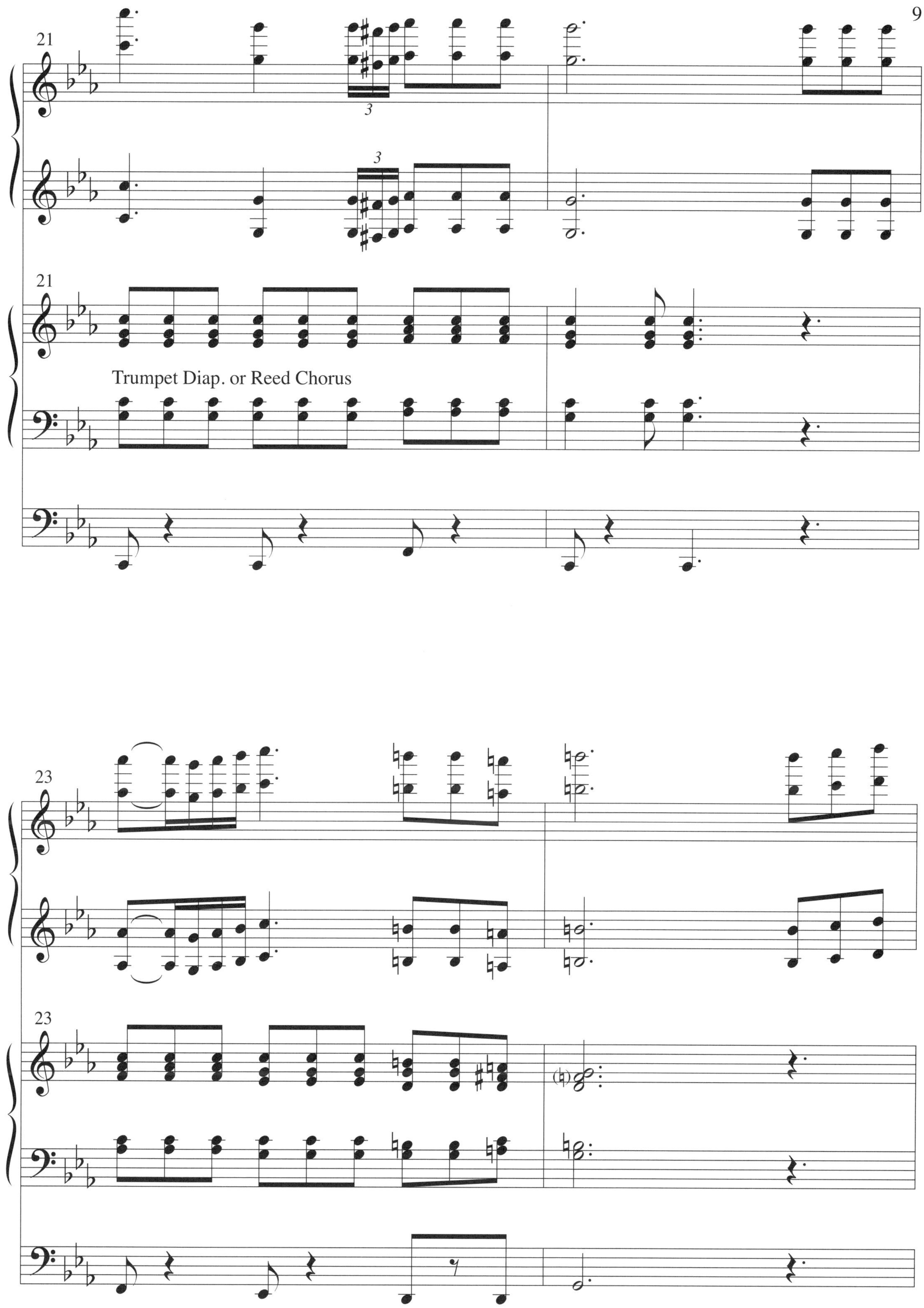

Trumpet Diap. or Reed Chorus

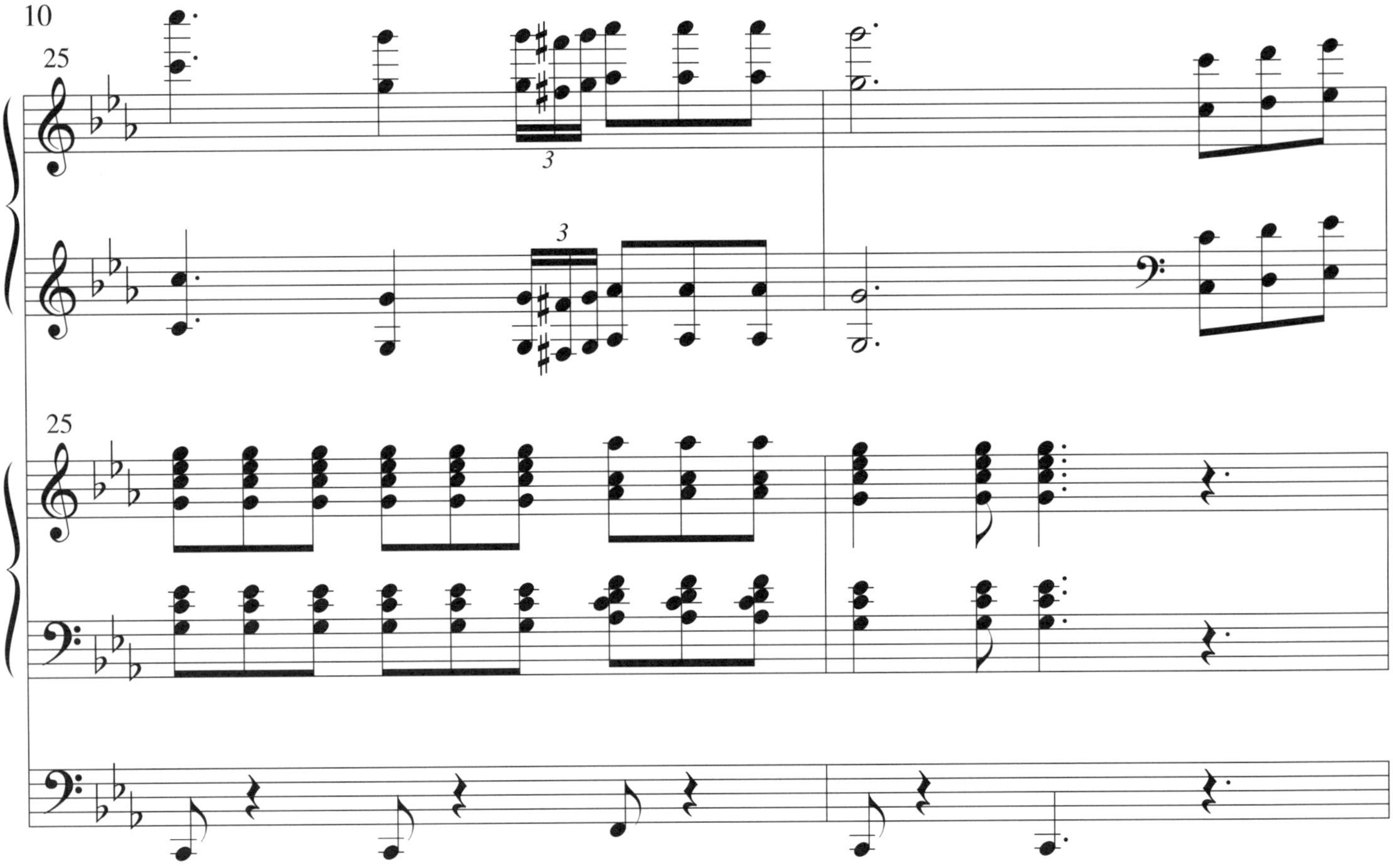

Slowly, deliberate

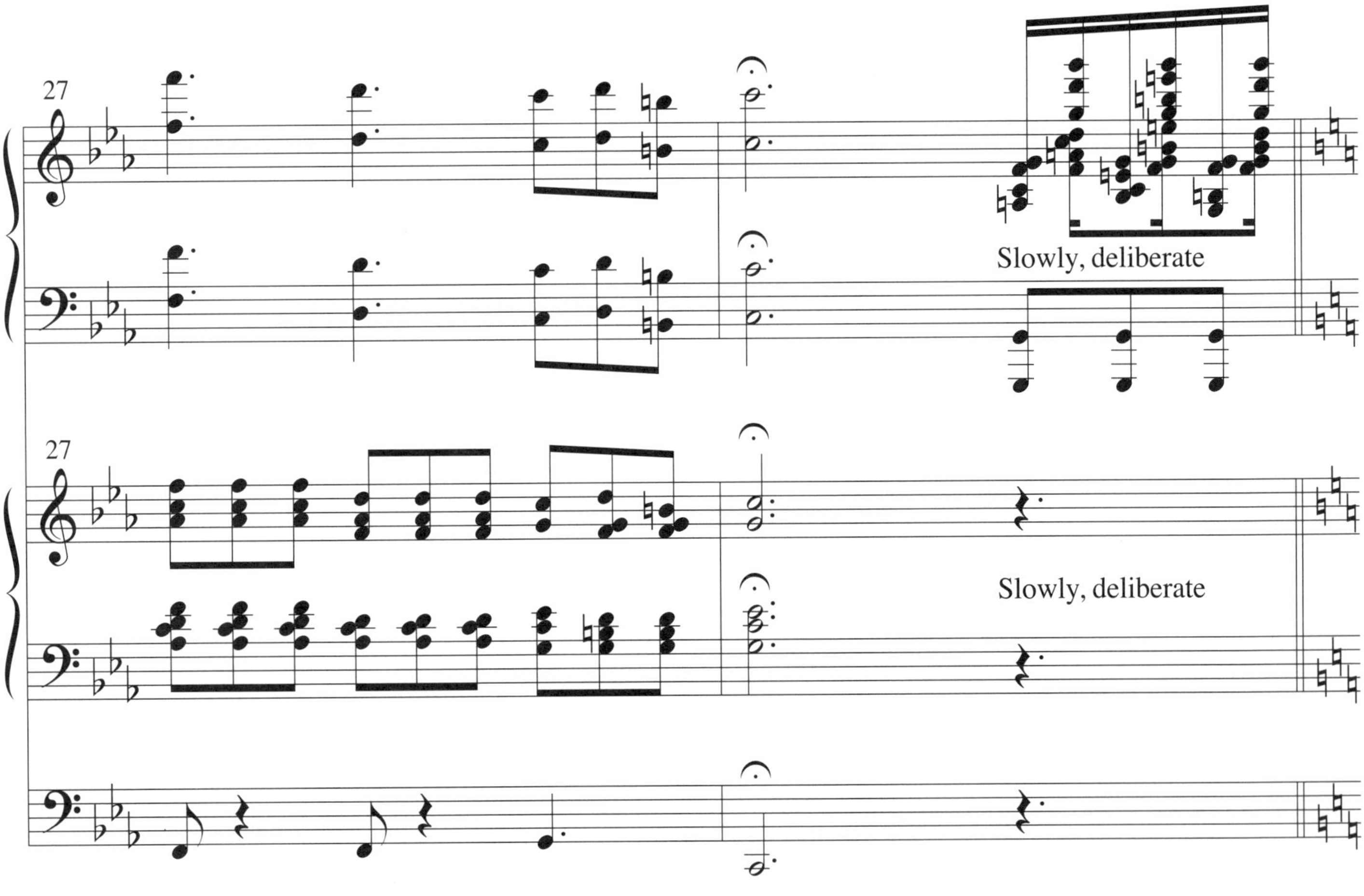

Slowly, deliberate

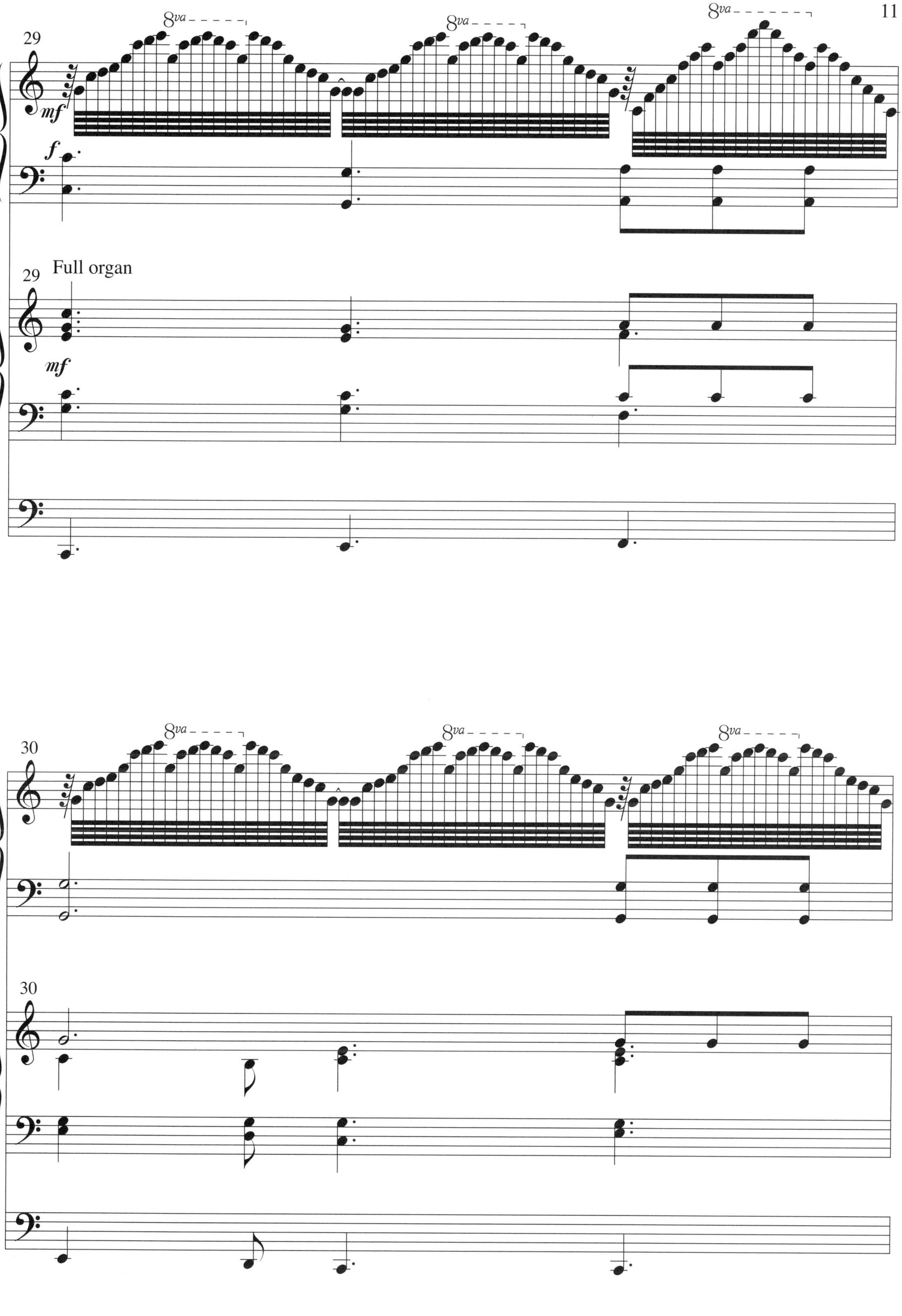
29
8va
mf
f
29 Full organ
mf
30
8va
30

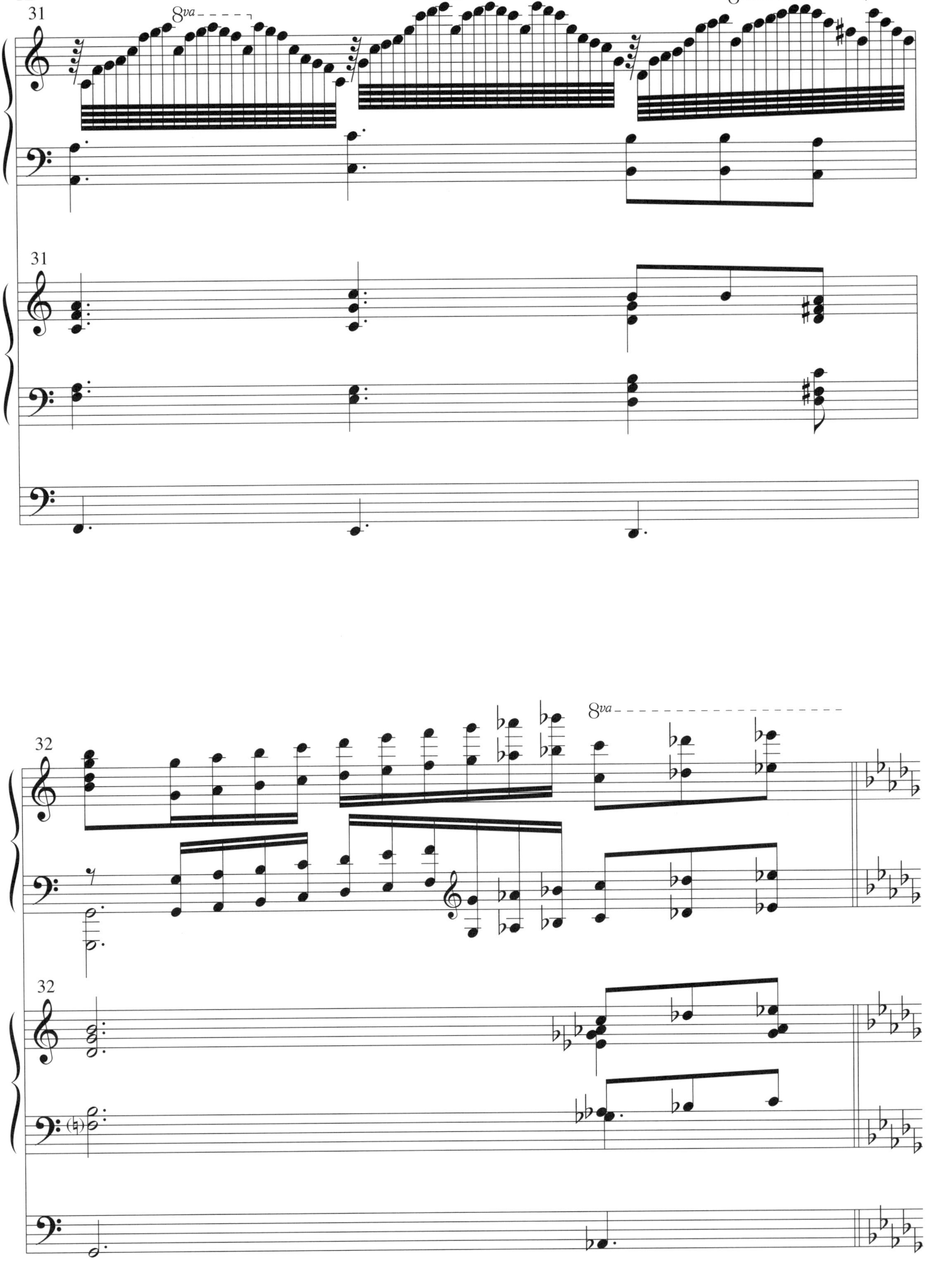
31
8va
8va
8va
31
32
8va
32

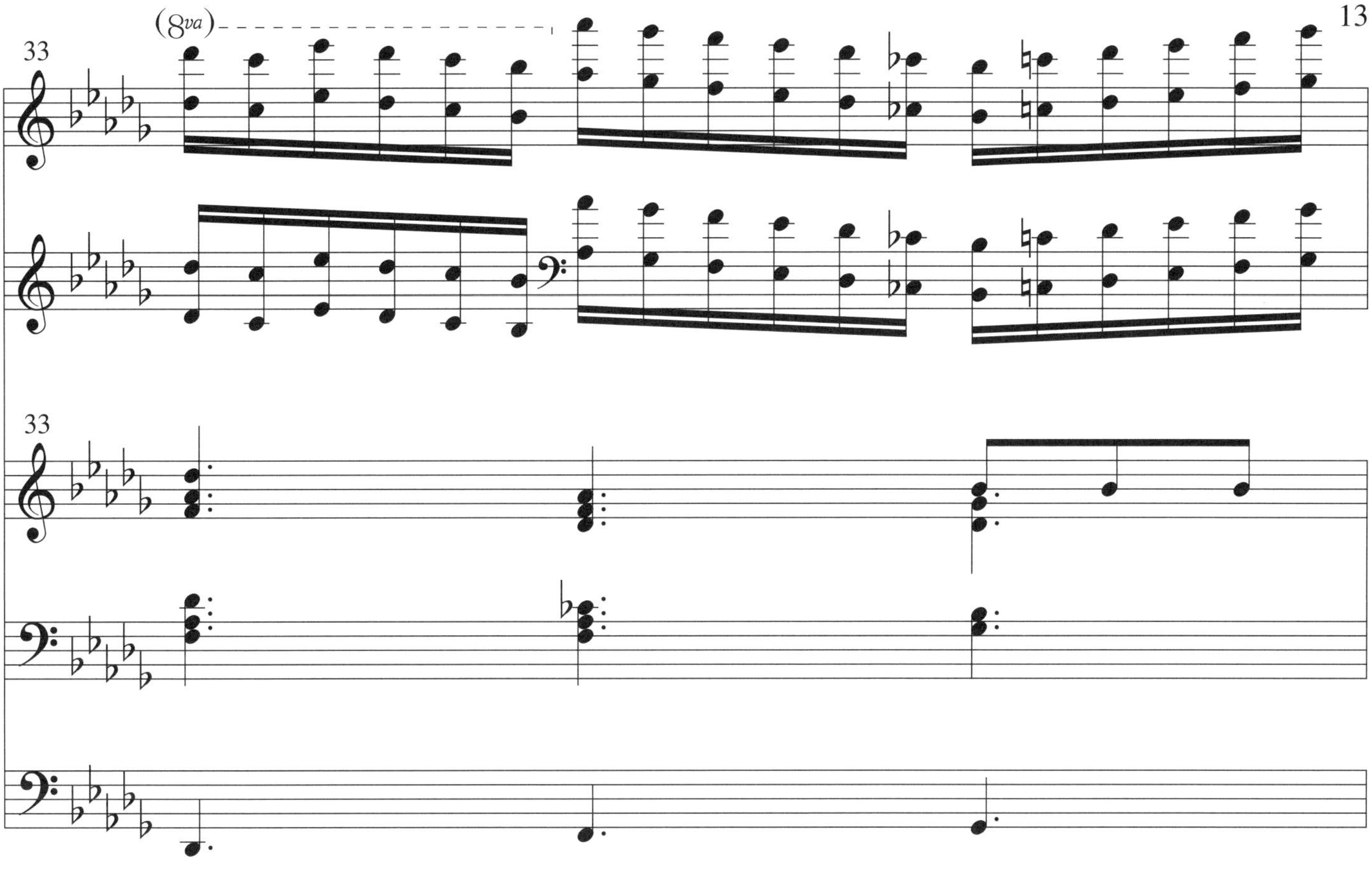
(8va)
33
33

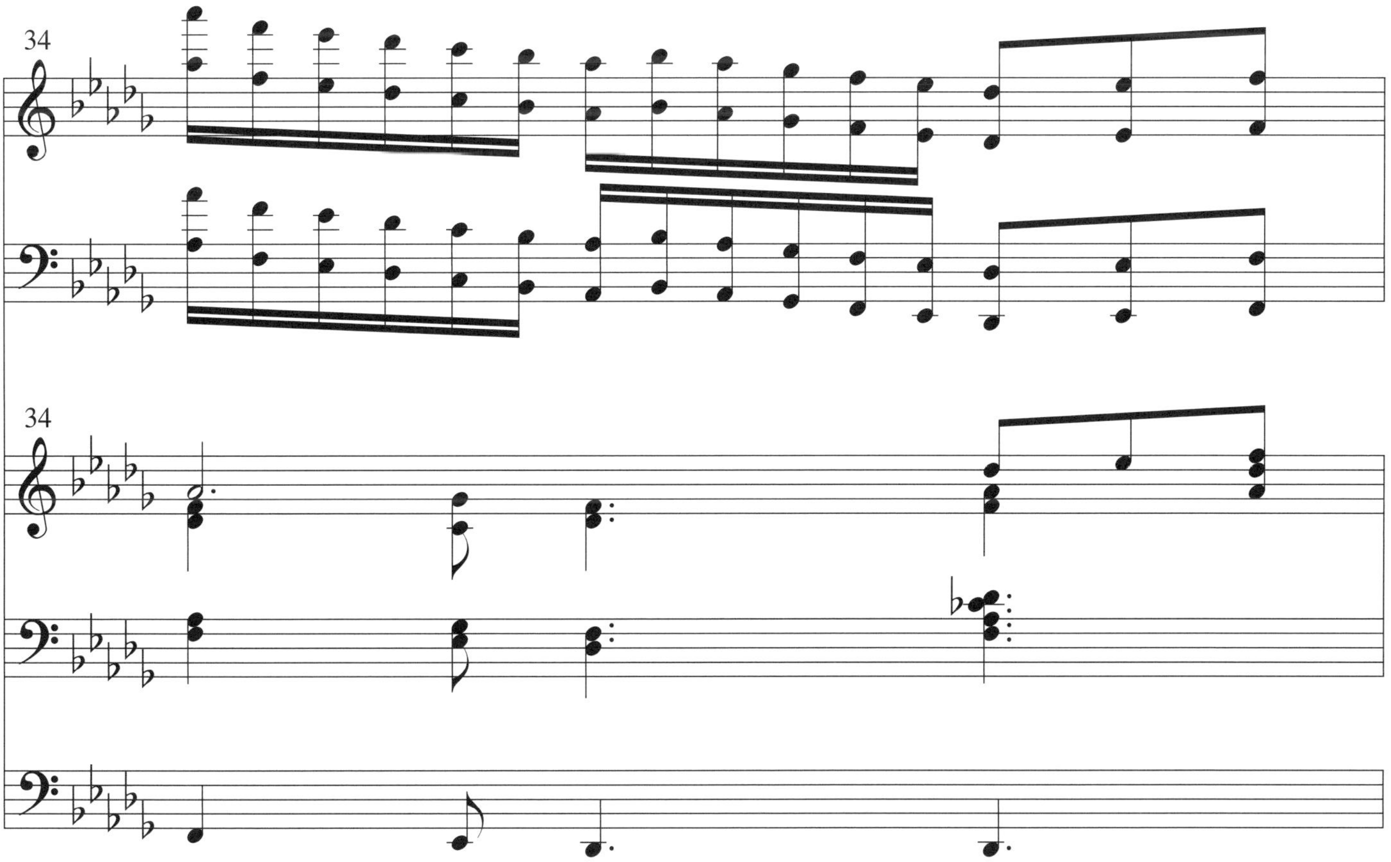
34
34

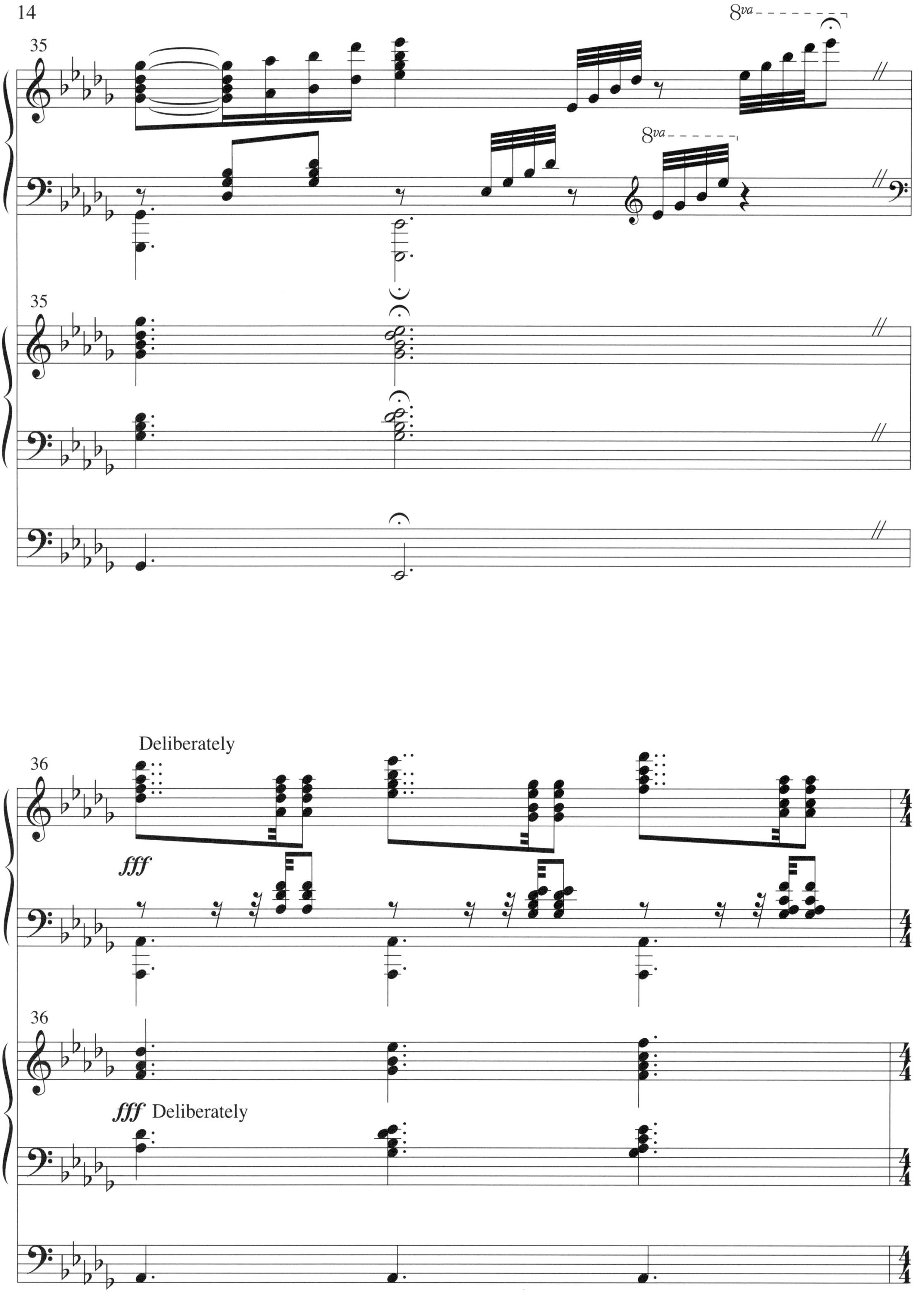
35
8va
8va
35
36
Deliberately
fff
36
fff Deliberately

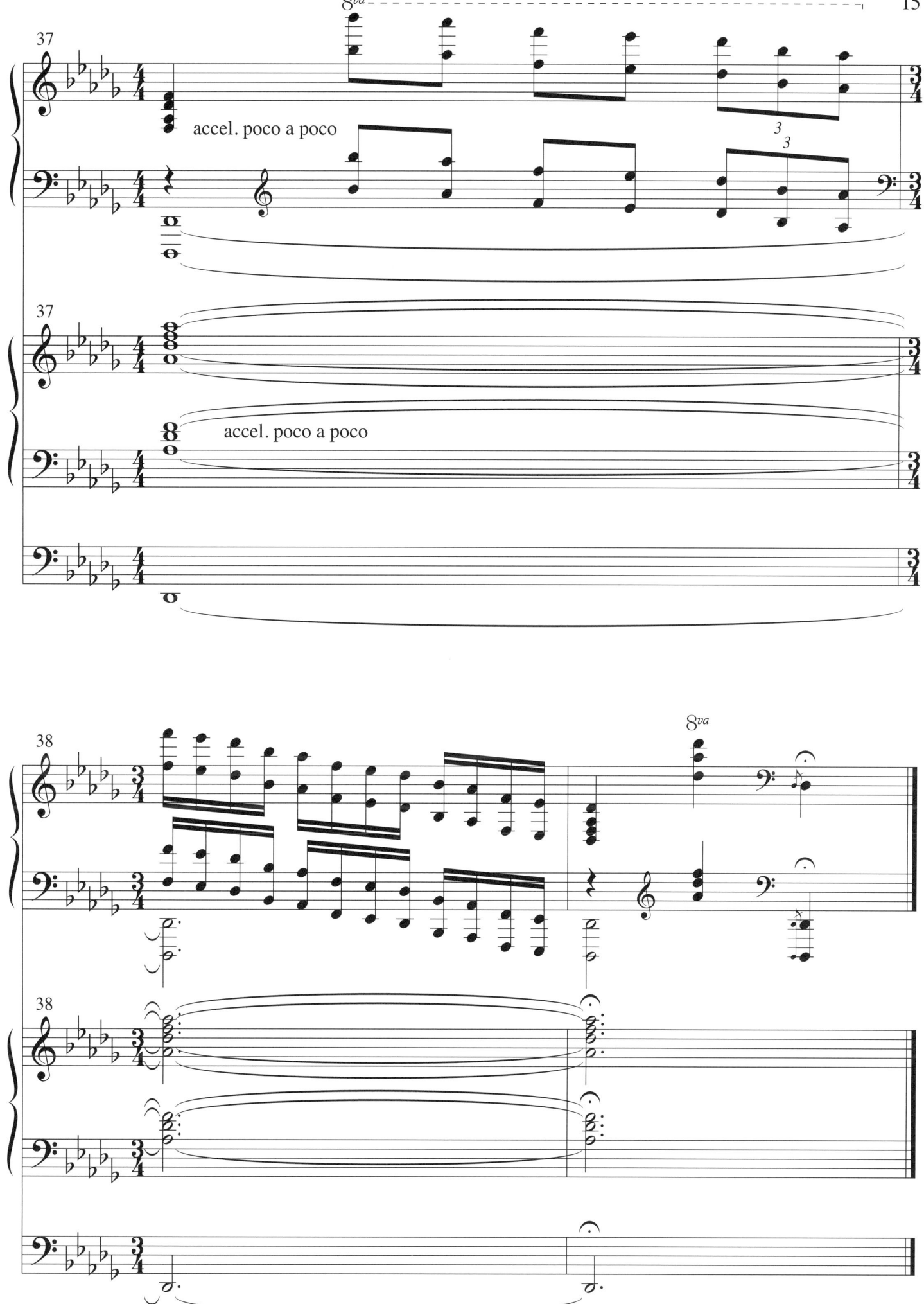

Wonderful Grace of Jesus

Sw. Gedeckt 8', Flute 4' 2', String 8'
Gt. Principal 8' 4' 2'
Ped. Bourdon 16', Octave 8'

HALDOR LILLENAS
Arranged by Paul Ferrin

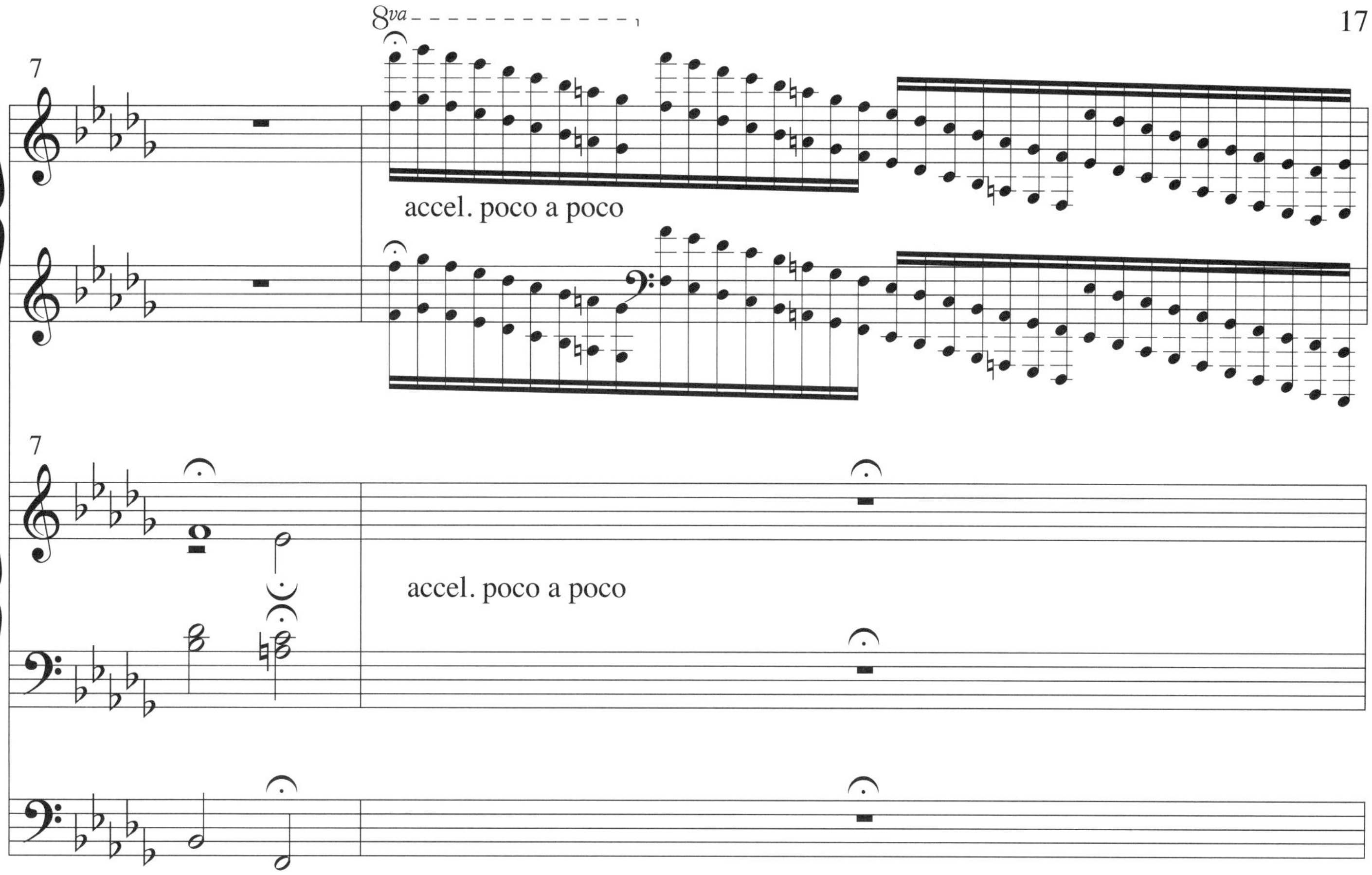
7
8va
accel. poco a poco
7
accel. poco a poco

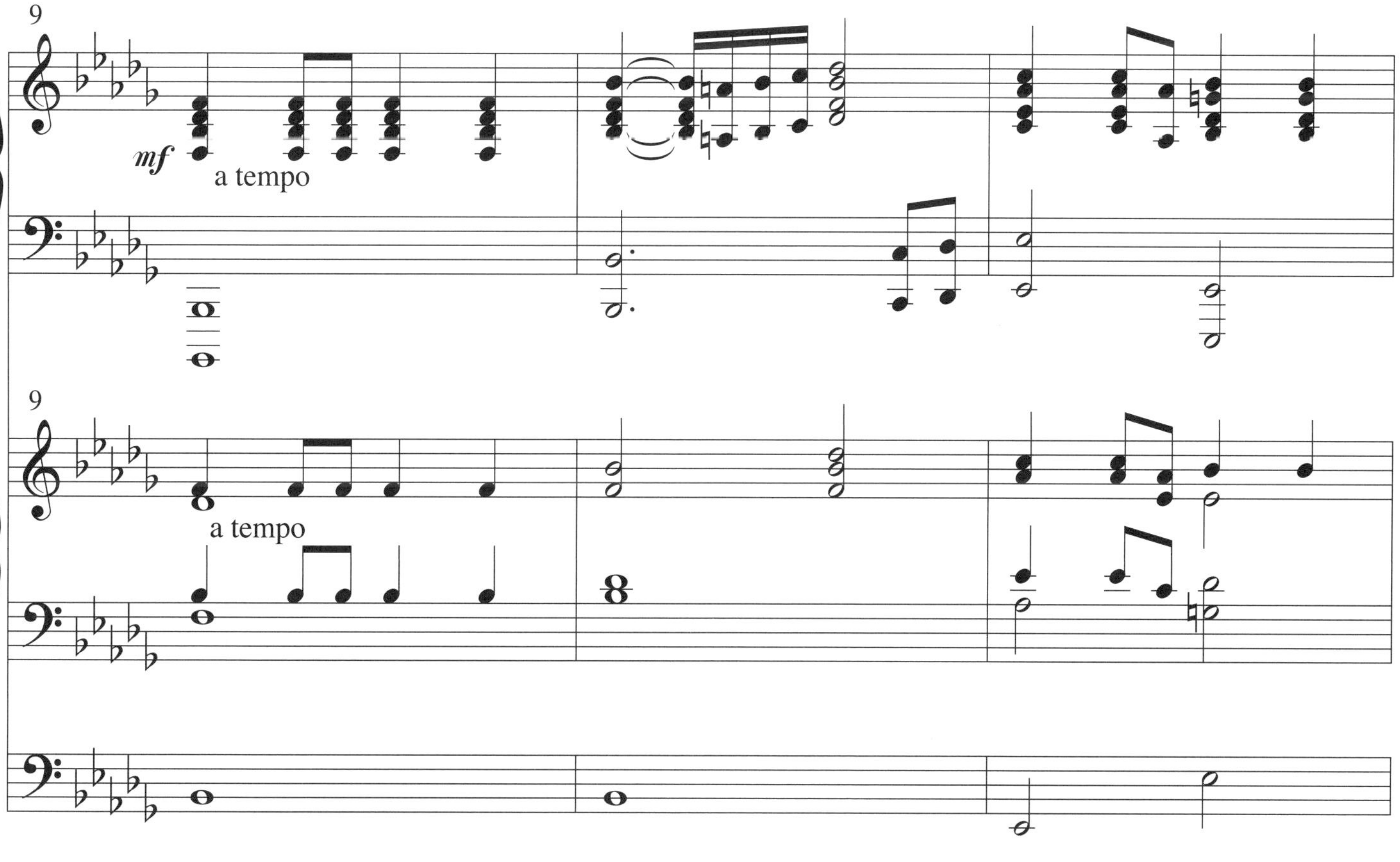
9
mf
a tempo
9
a tempo

12
rit.
(13)
Joyously ♩ = ca. 120
f
12
Sw. to Gt.
+Flute 8' 4'
rit.
f Faster
14
3
14

Sw. Trumpet

Gt. Full Organ

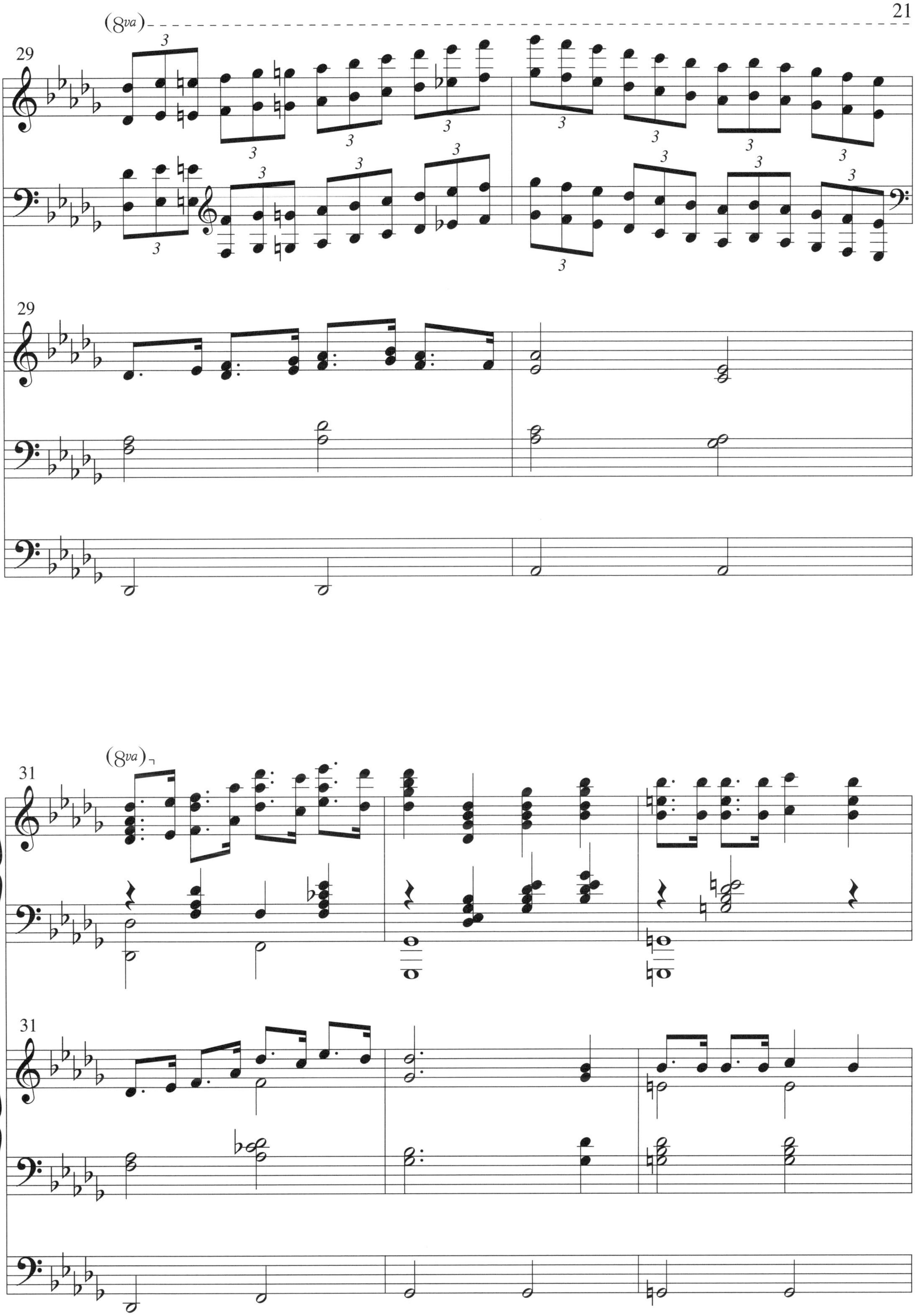
(8va)
29
29
(8va)
31
31

34
3
3
34
36
8va
rit.
17
Slower ♩ = ca. 70
8va
mf
36
Principal 8' 4' 2'
rit.
mf Slower

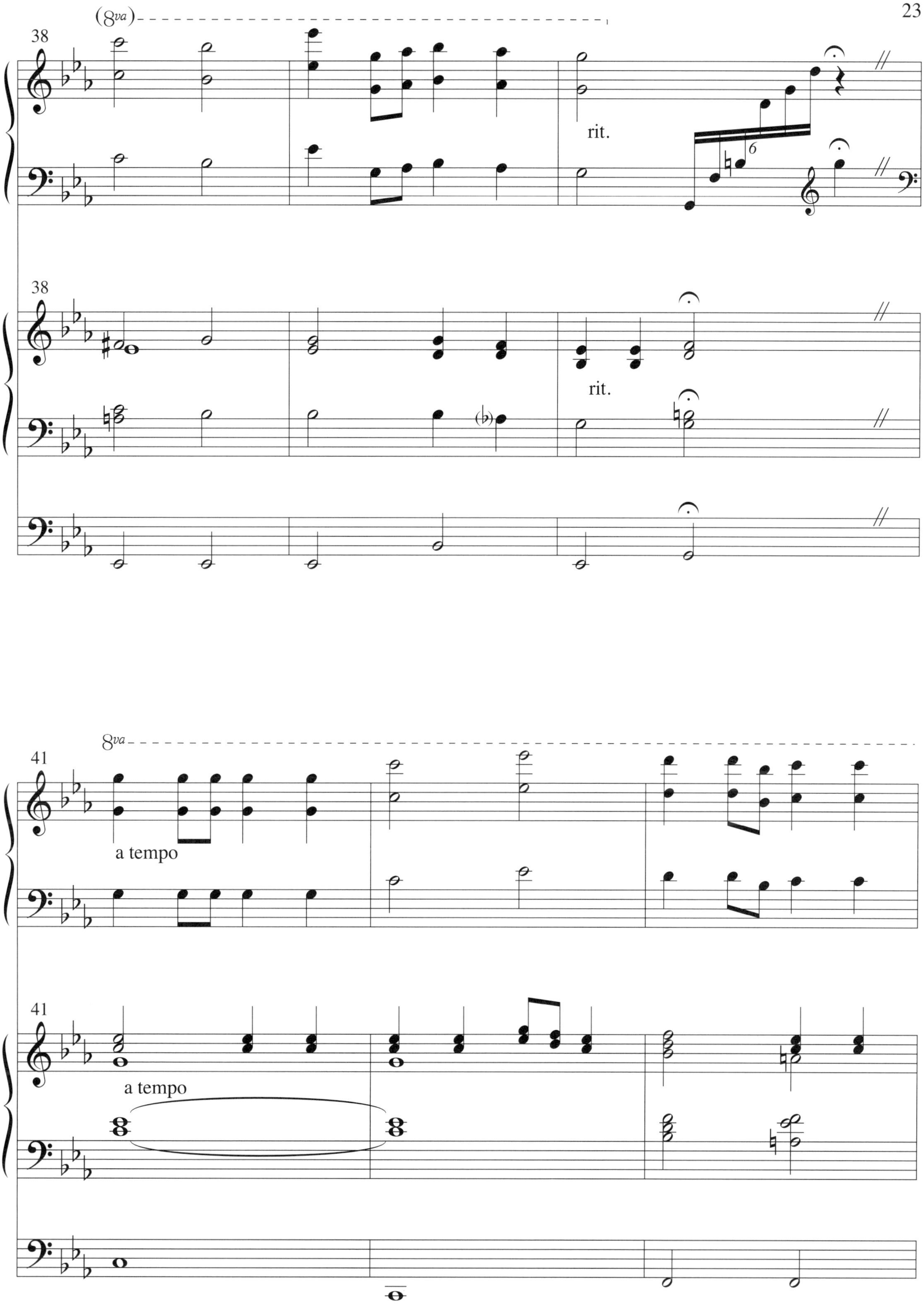
(8va)
38
rit.
6
38
rit.
8va
41
a tempo
41
a tempo

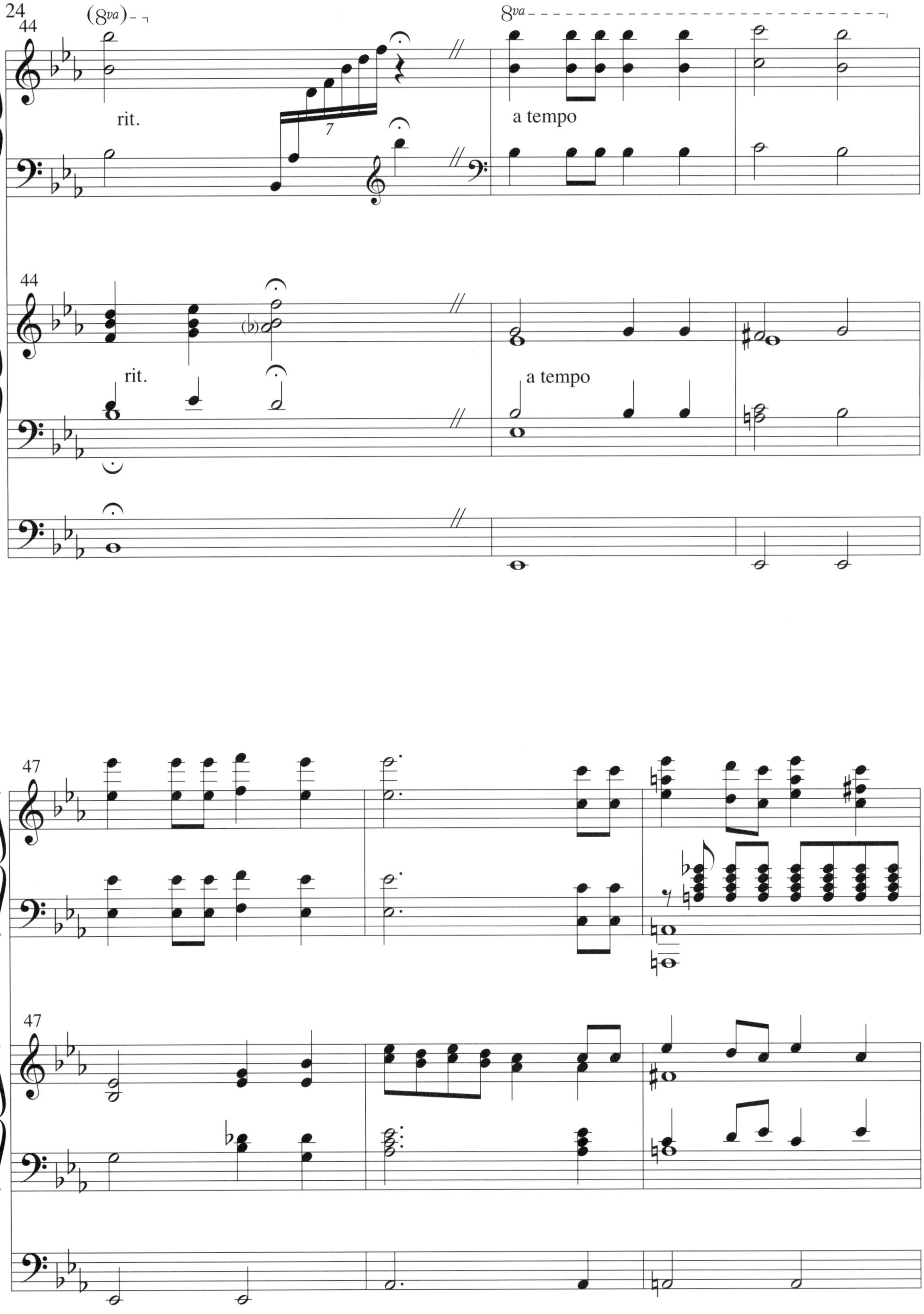
44
(8va)
8va
rit.
7
a tempo
44
rit.
a tempo
47
47

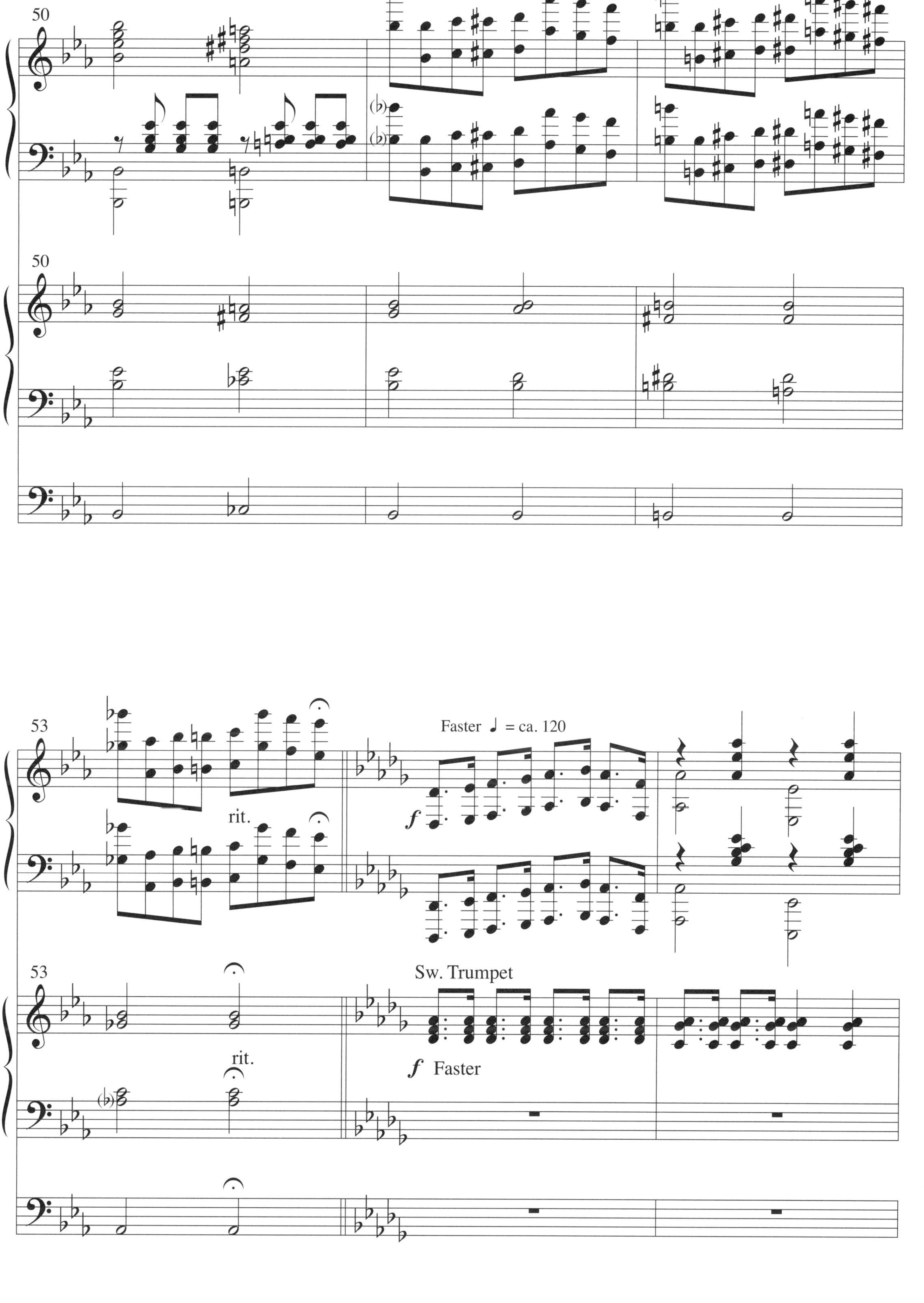
50
50
53
rit.
Faster ♩ = ca. 120
f
53
rit.
Sw. Trumpet
f Faster

Gt. Full Organ

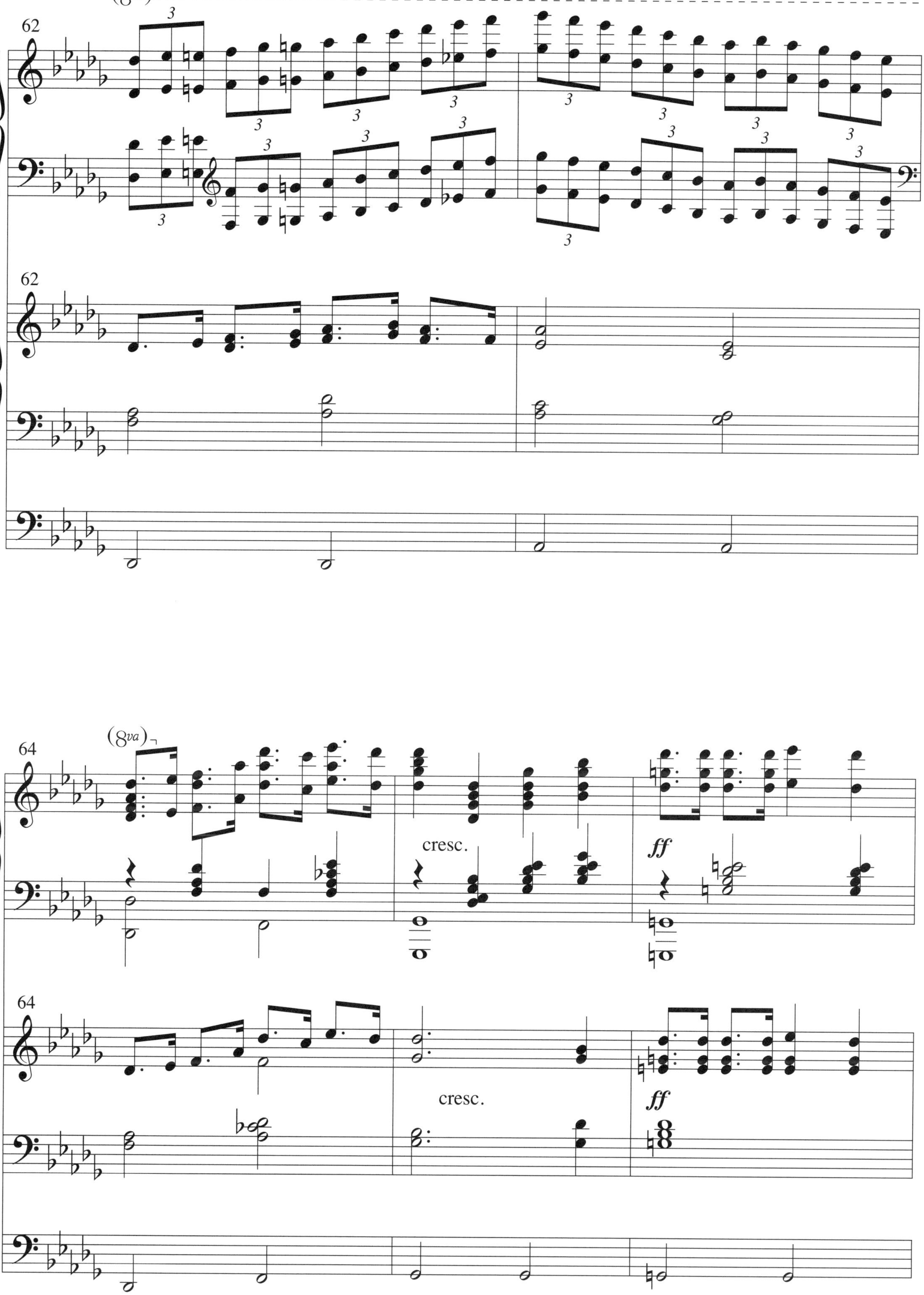
(8va)
62
62
(8va)
64
cresc.
ff
64
cresc.
ff

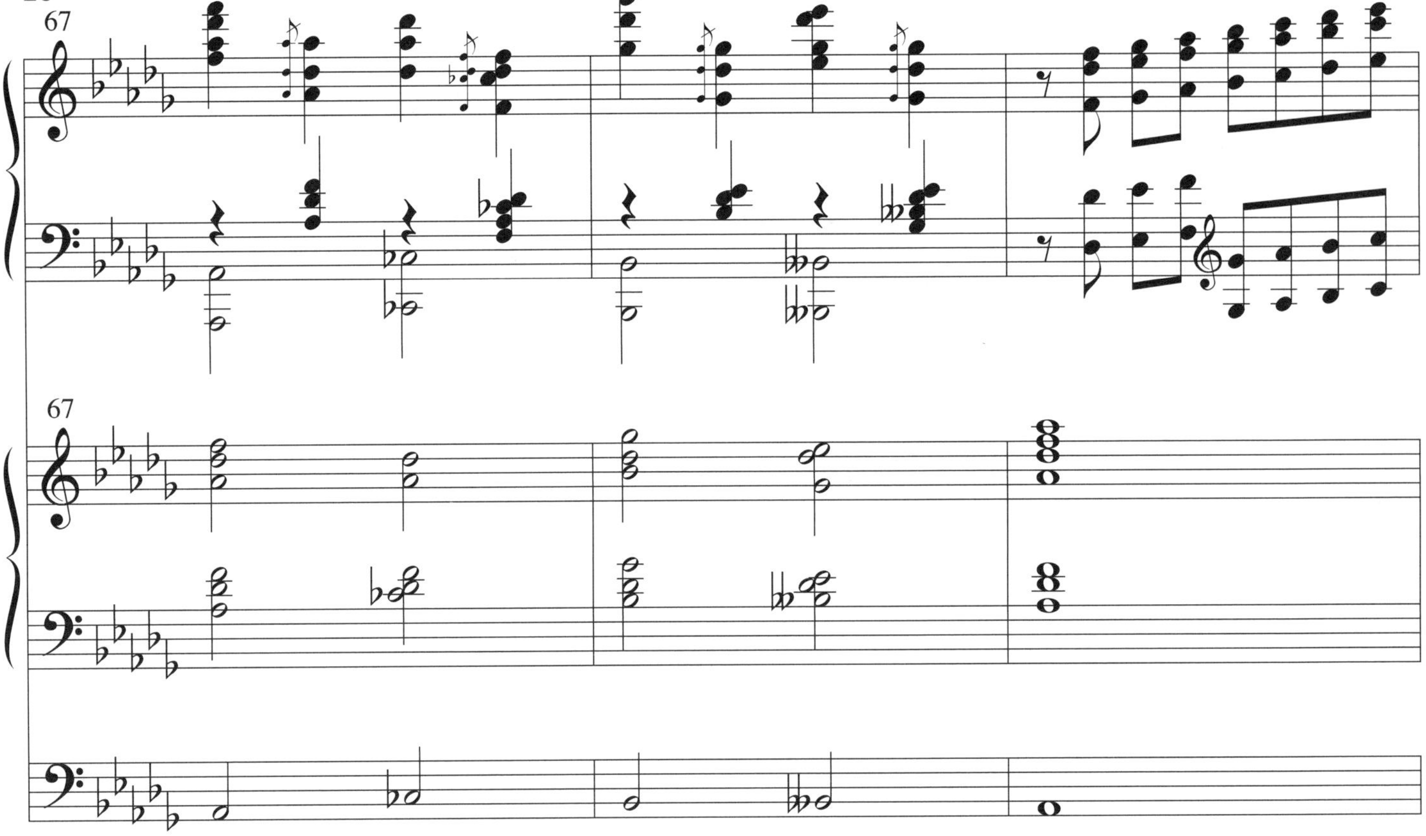
67
67

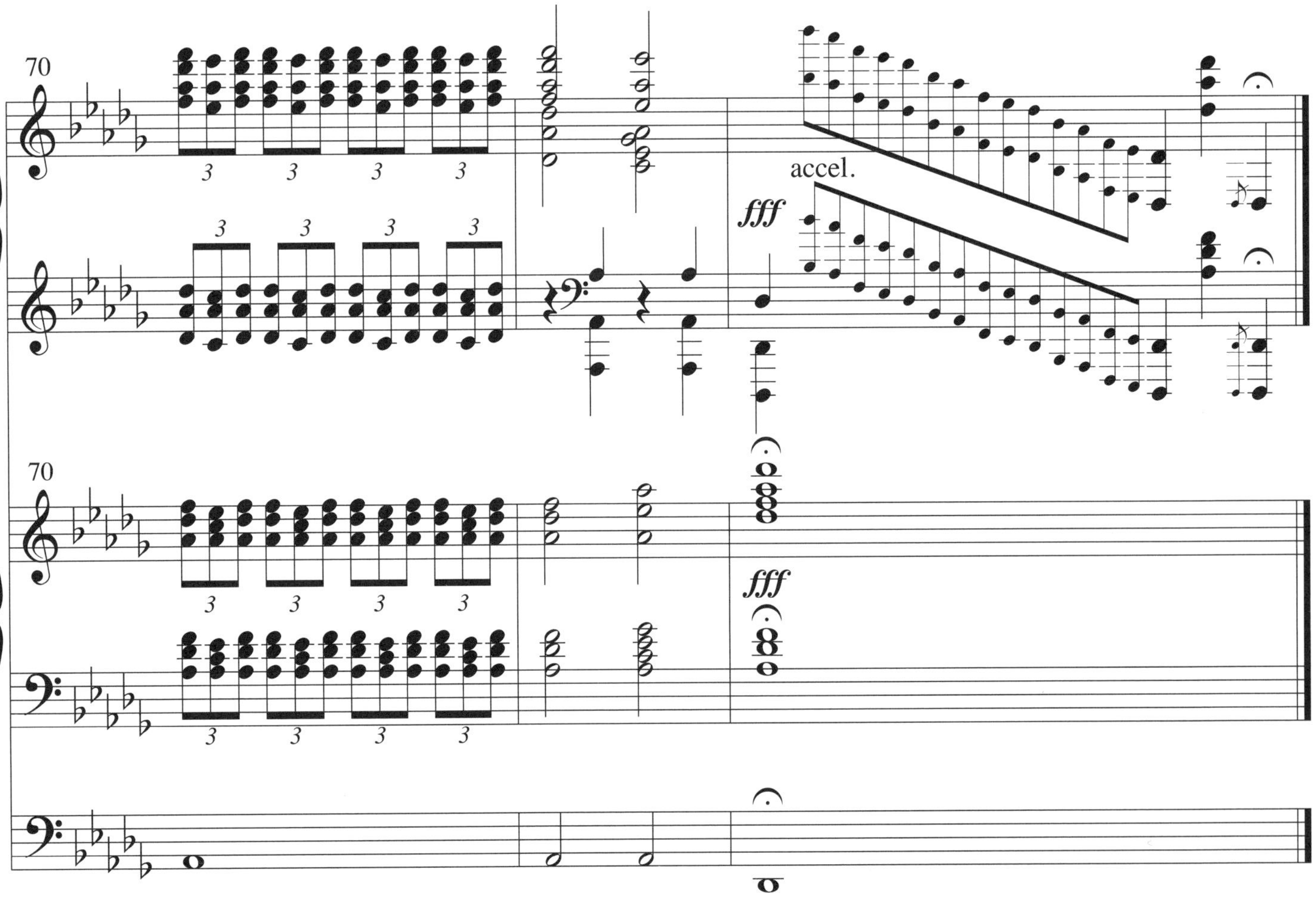
70
accel.
fff
70
fff

Come and Dine

Sw. Flutes 8', 4', 2'
Gt. Principal 8', 4', 2'
Ped. Principal 16', 8'

C. B. WIDMEYER
Arranged by Paul Ferrin

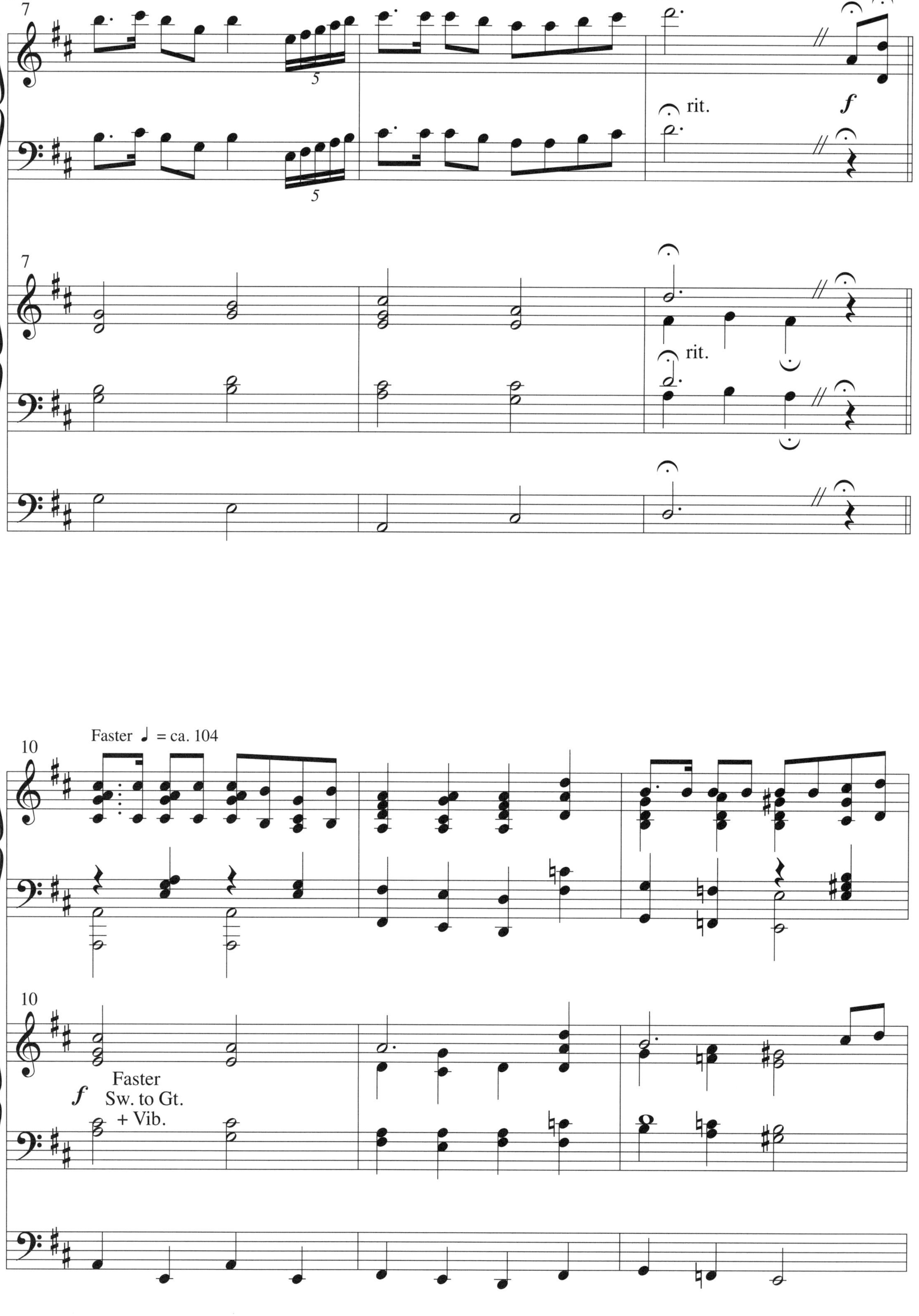
7
5
5
rit.
f
7
rit.
10
Faster ♩ = ca. 104
10
f
Faster
Sw. to Gt.
+ Vib.

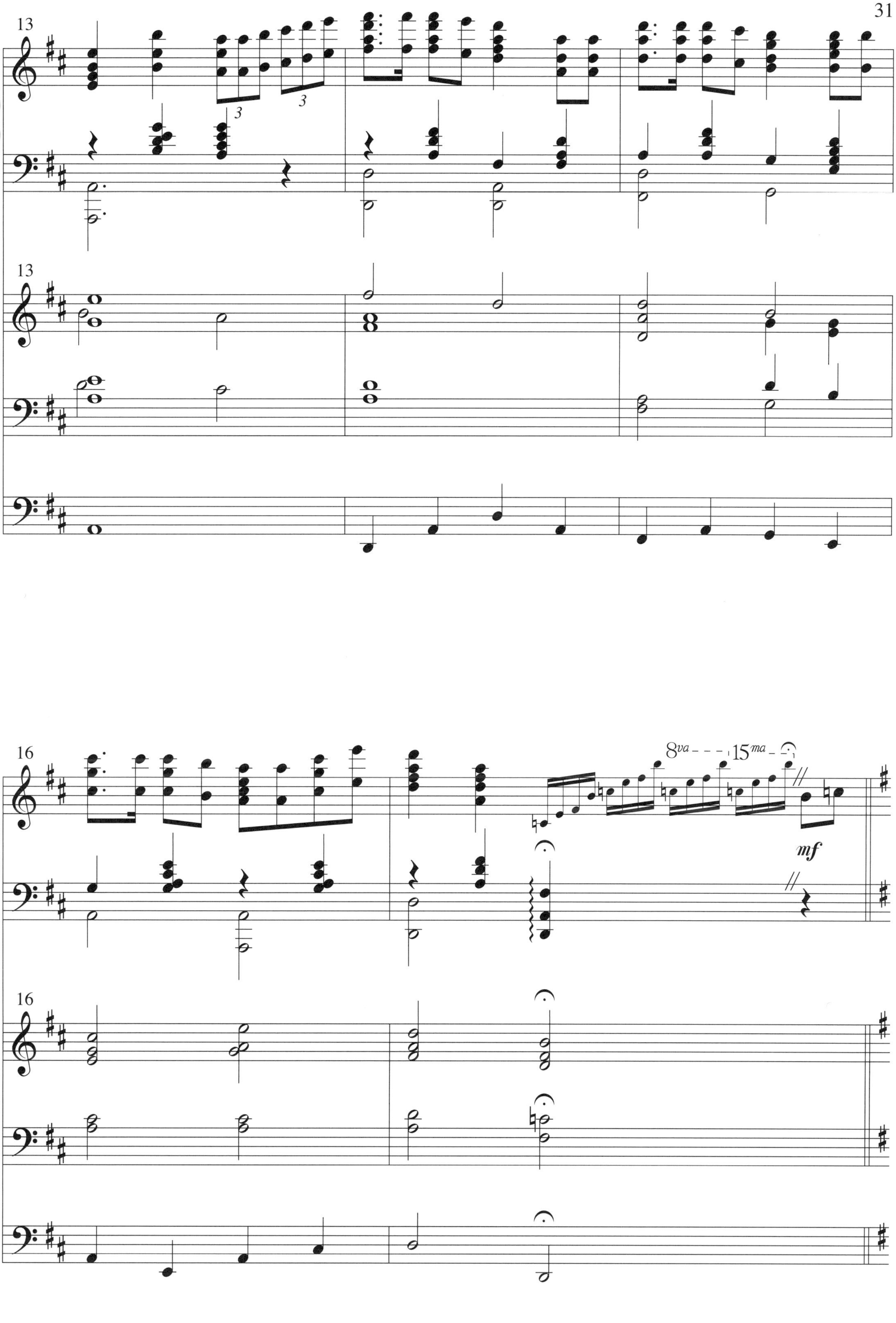
13
3
3
13
16
8va
15ma
mf
16

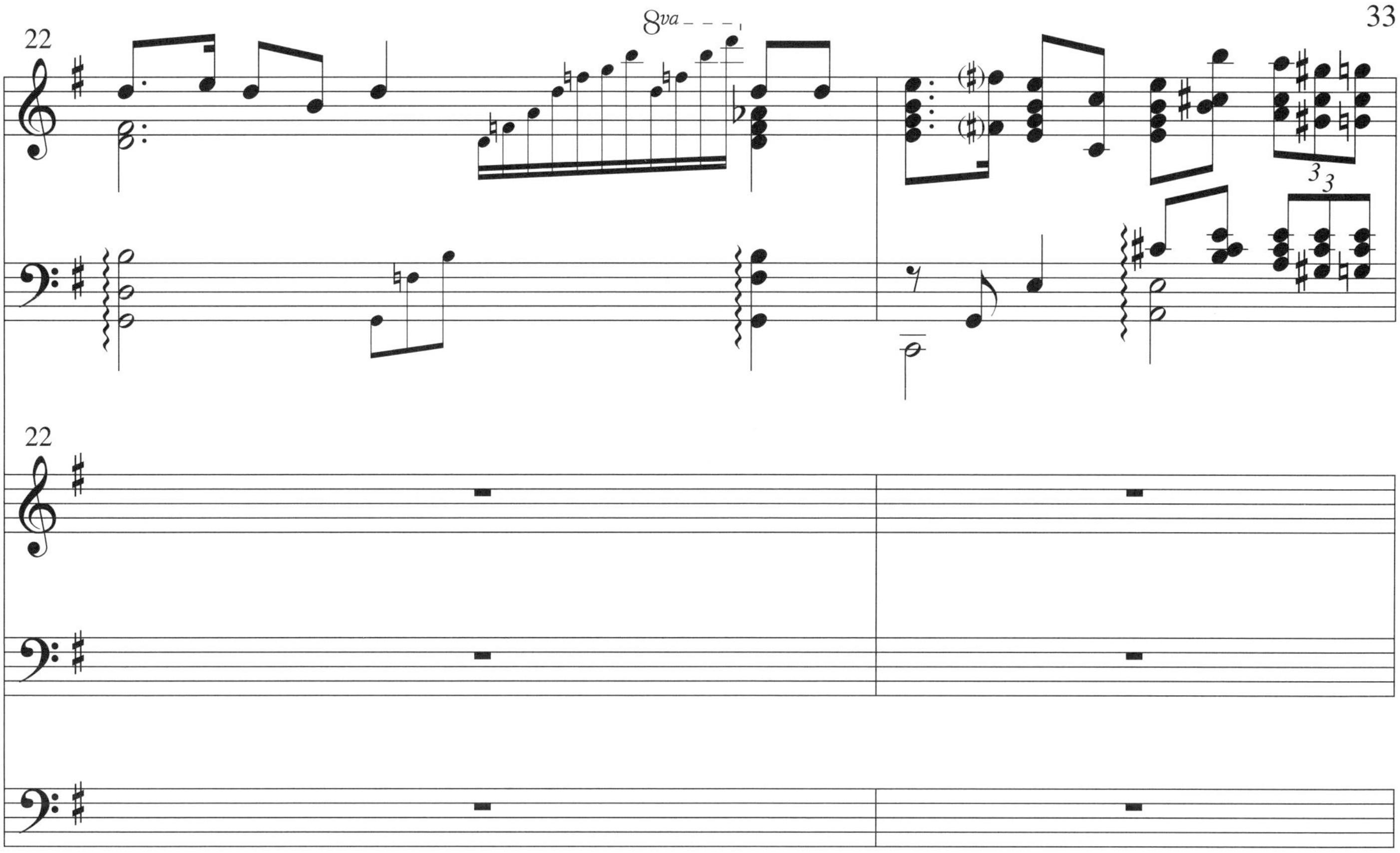

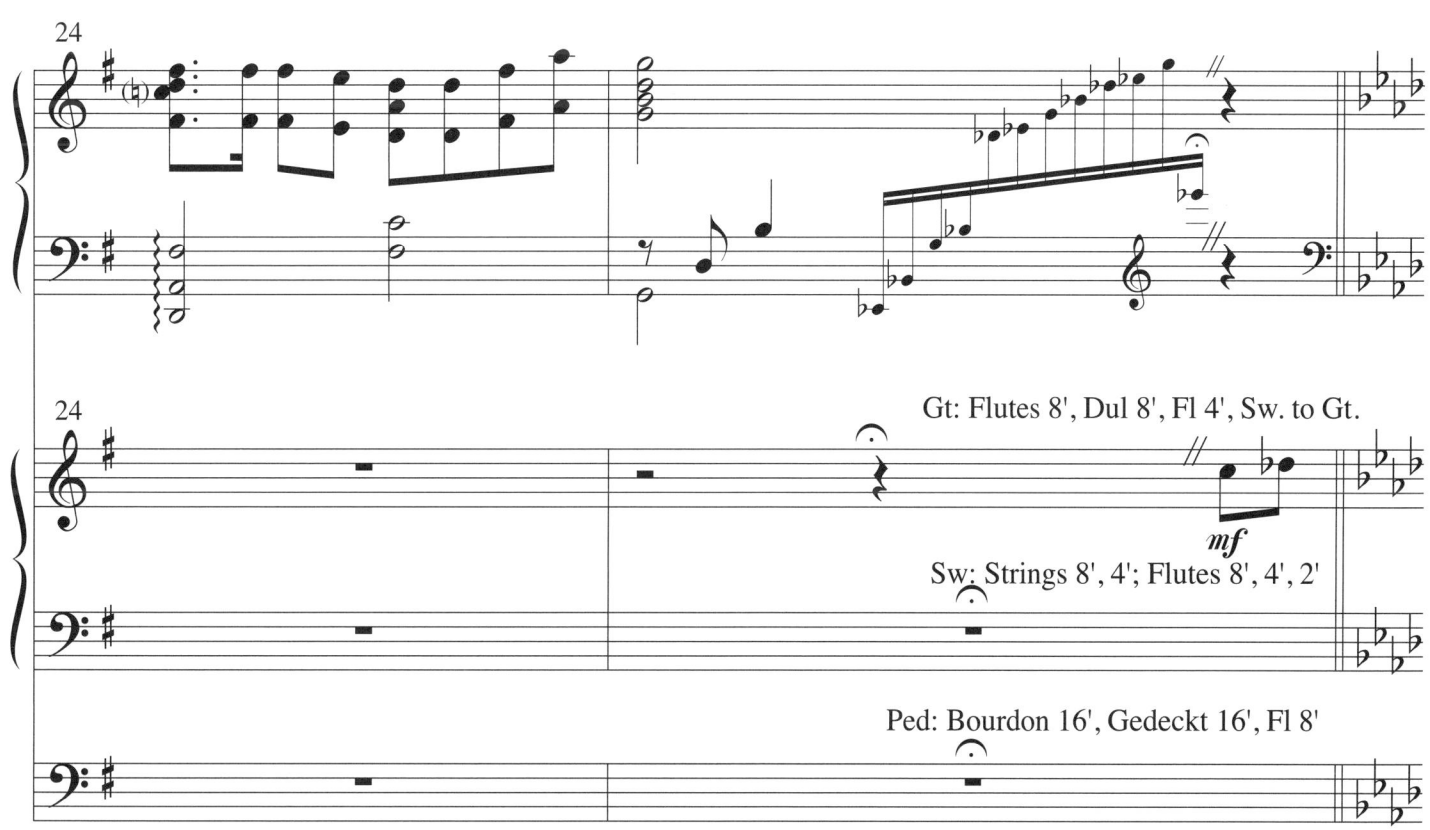

Gt: Flutes 8', Dul 8', Fl 4', Sw. to Gt.

Sw: Strings 8', 4'; Flutes 8', 4', 2'

Ped: Bourdon 16', Gedeckt 16', Fl 8'

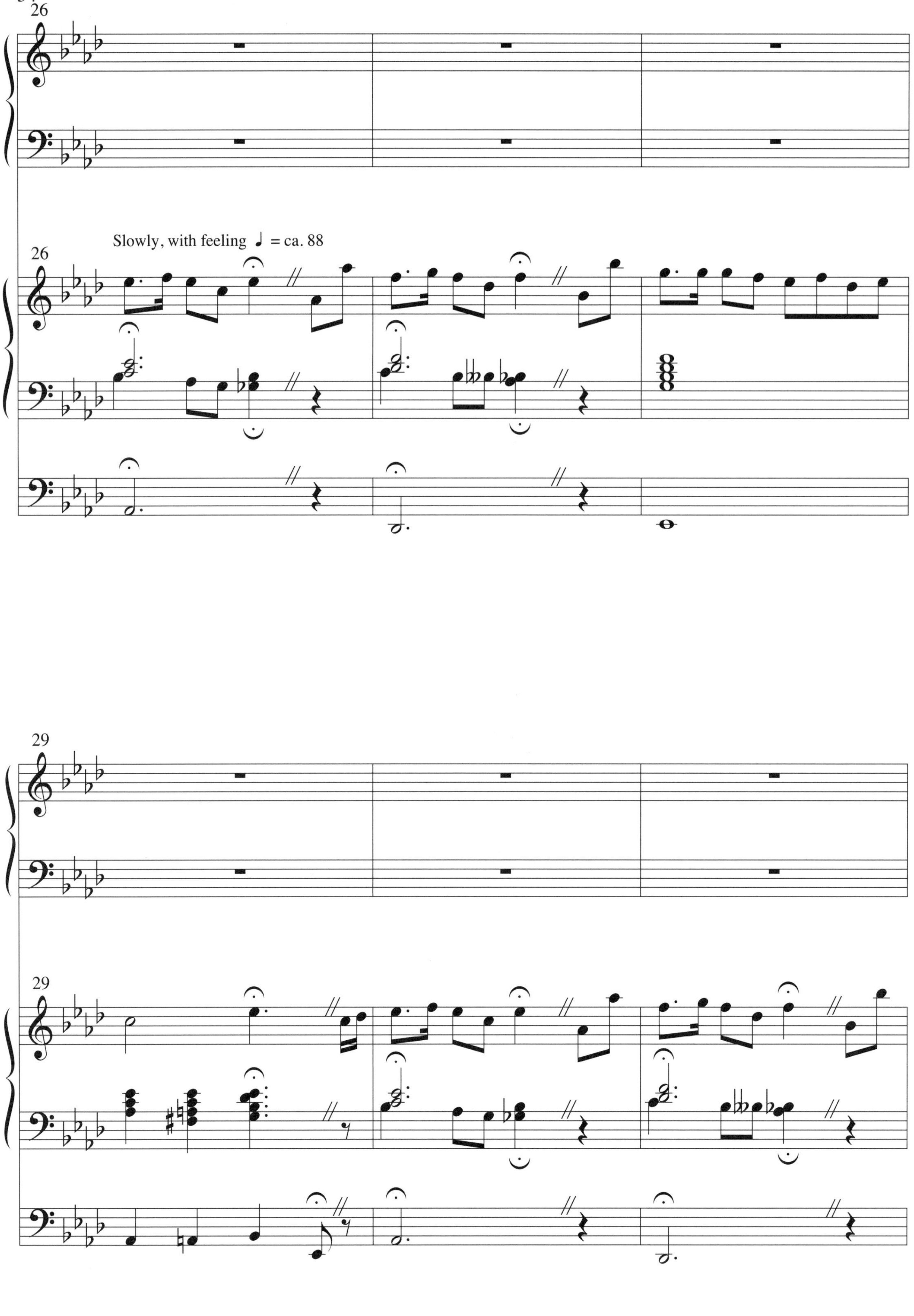
26
26
Slowly, with feeling ♩ = ca. 88
29
29

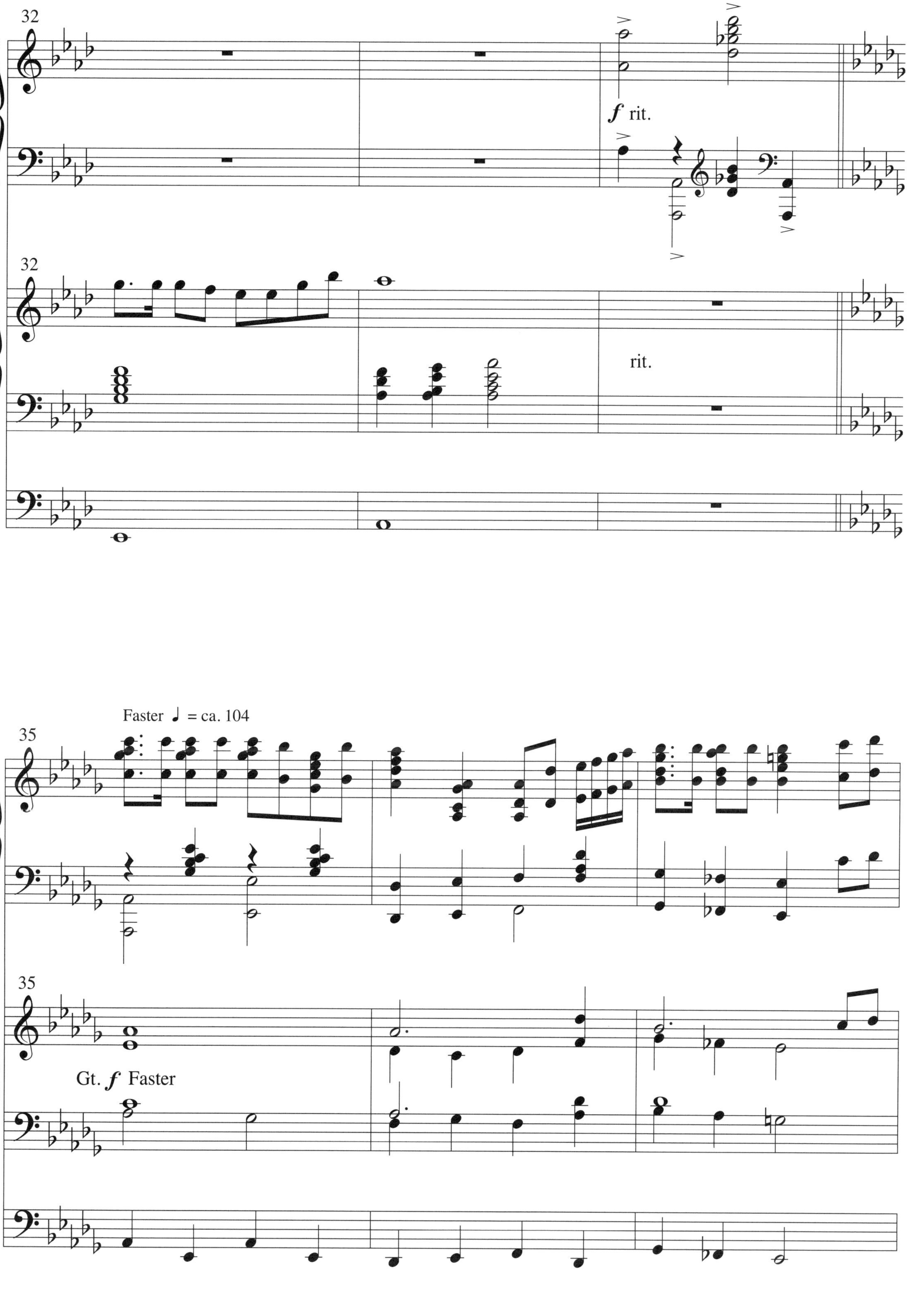
32
f rit.
32
rit.
Faster ♩ = ca. 104
35
35
Gt. f Faster

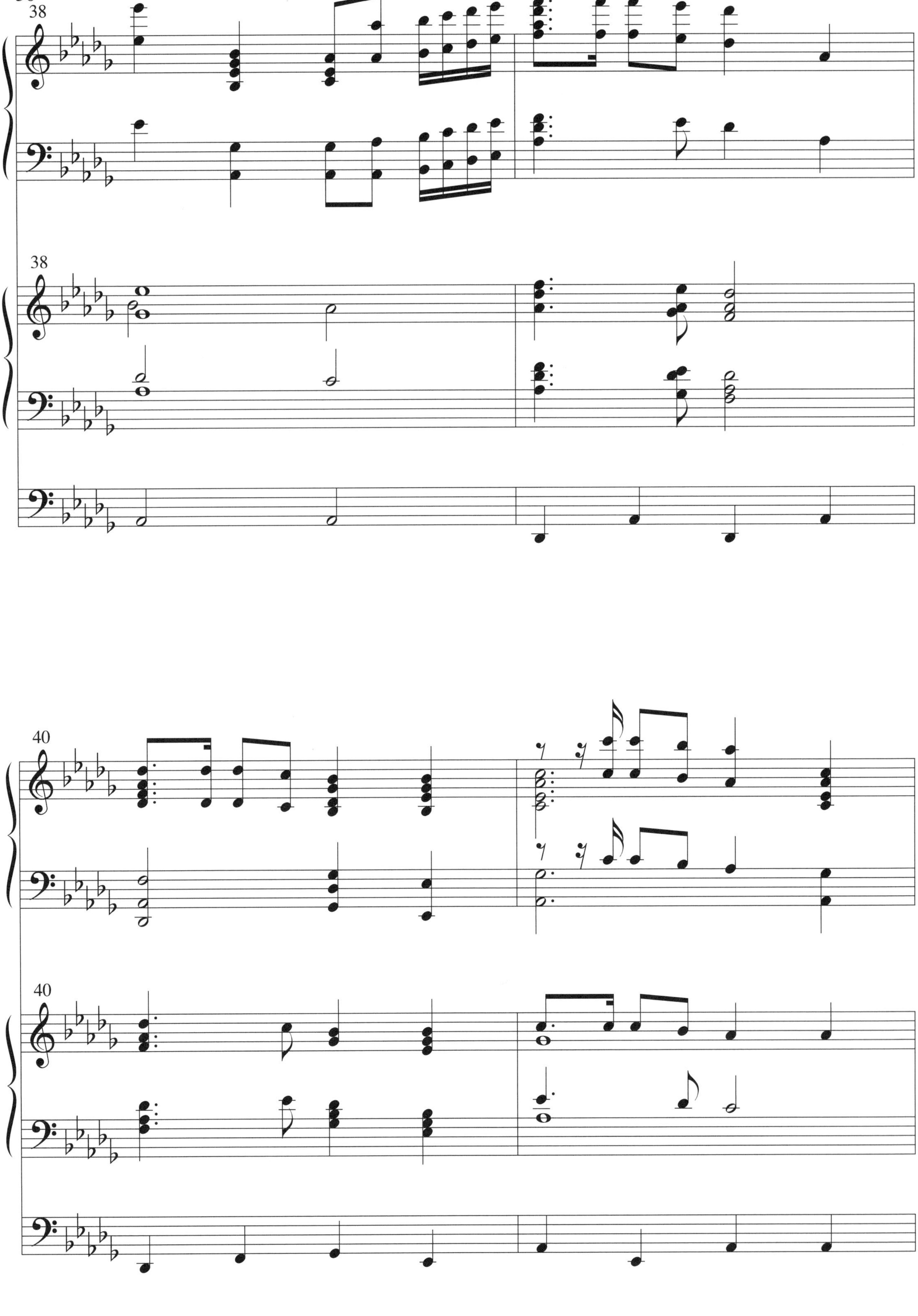

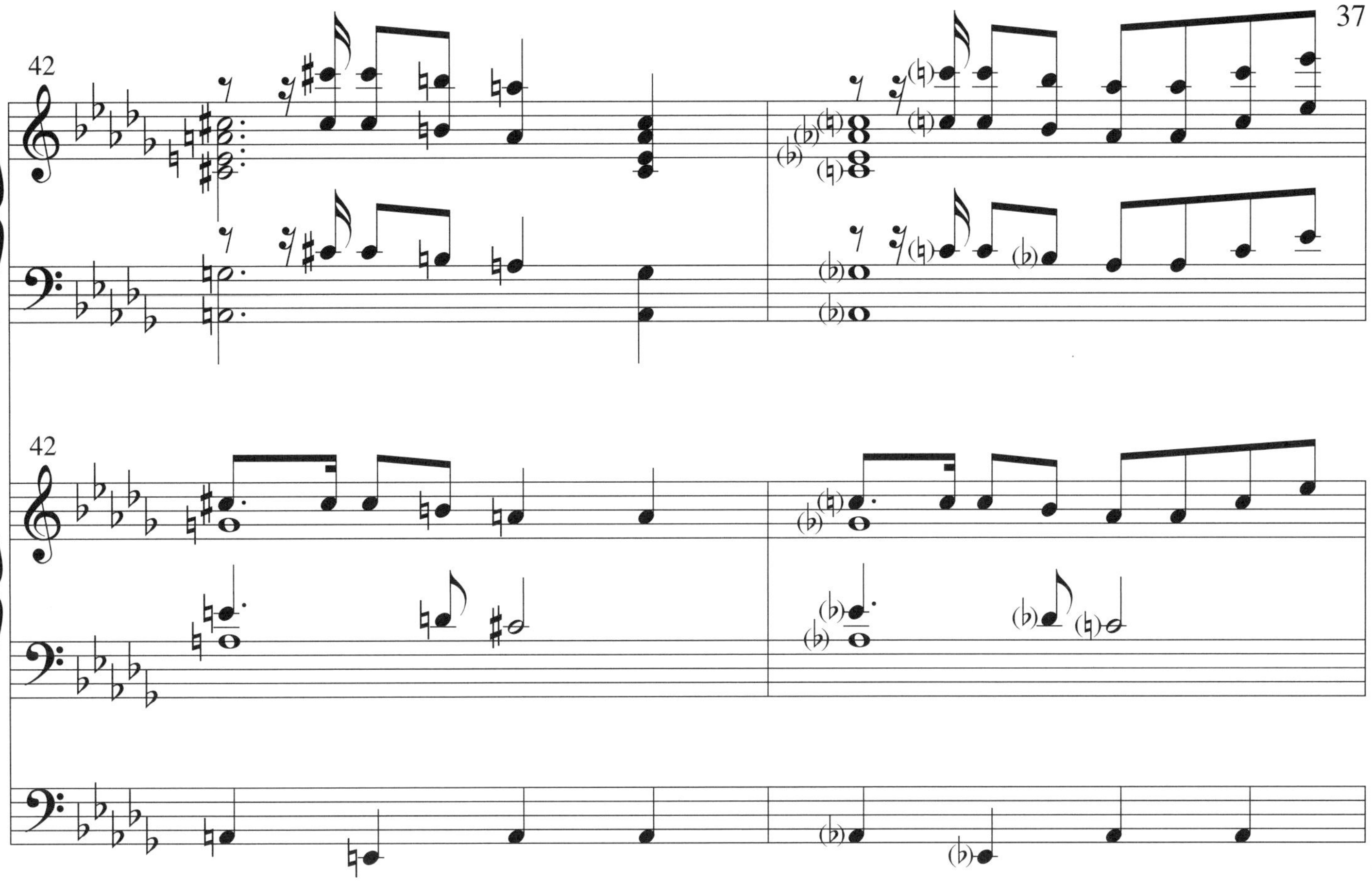
42
42

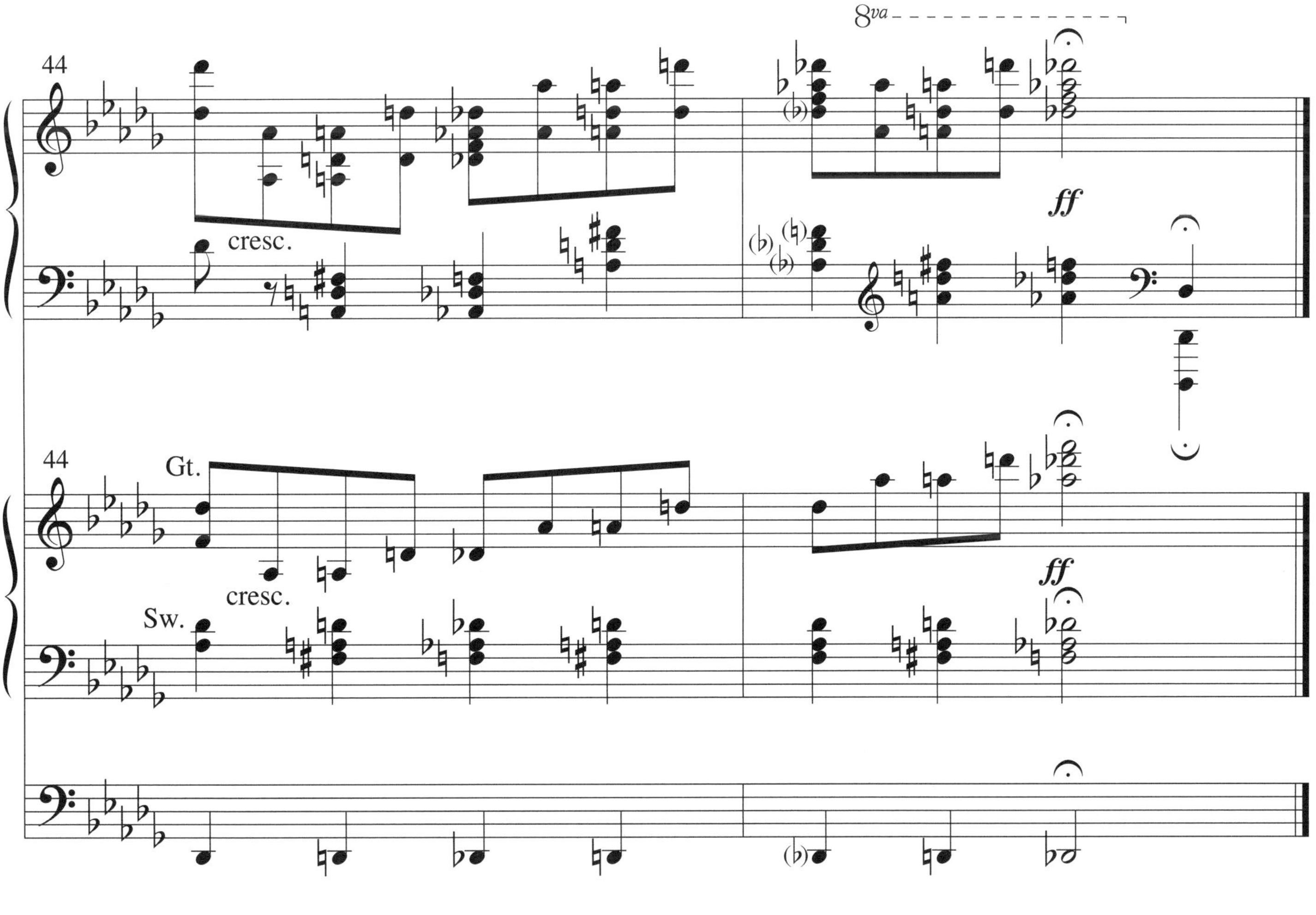
44
cresc.
8va
ff
44
Gt.
cresc.
Sw.
ff

Nearer, Still Nearer

Sw.   Strings 8' 4'
Gt.   Oboe 8', Flute 8'
Ped.   Gedeckt 16', Flute 8'

LELIA N. MORRIS
Arranged by Paul Ferrin

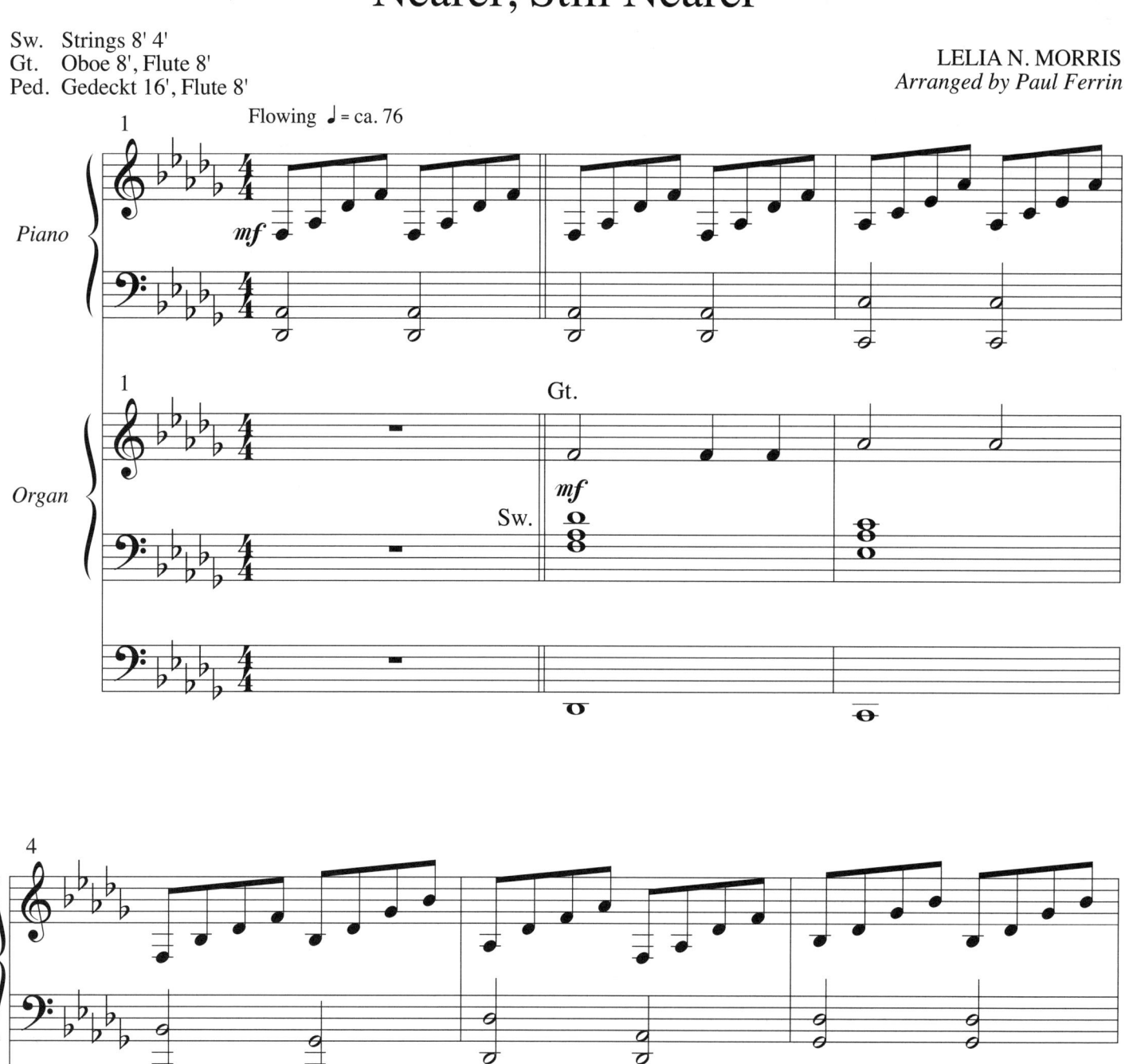

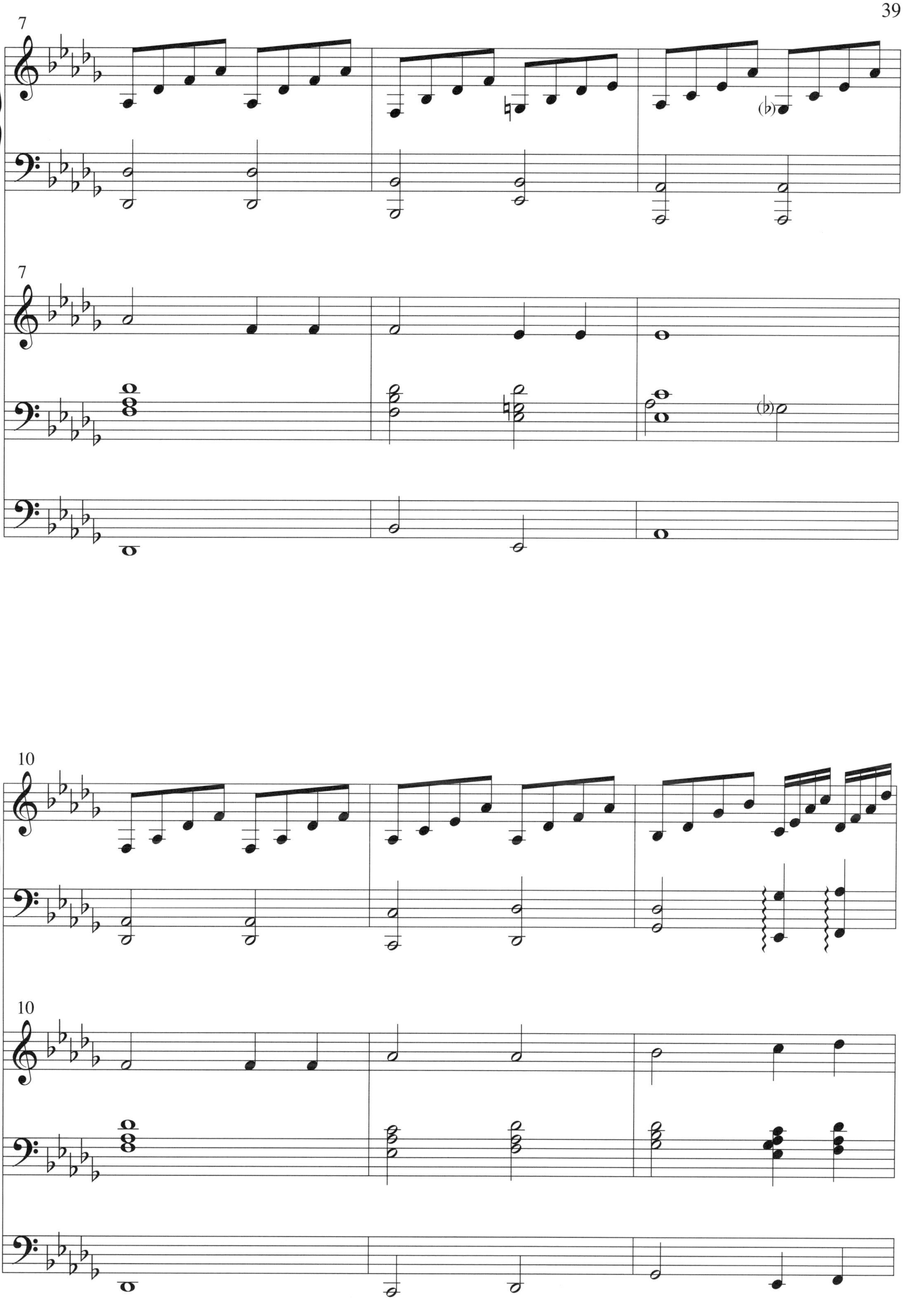
7
7
10
10

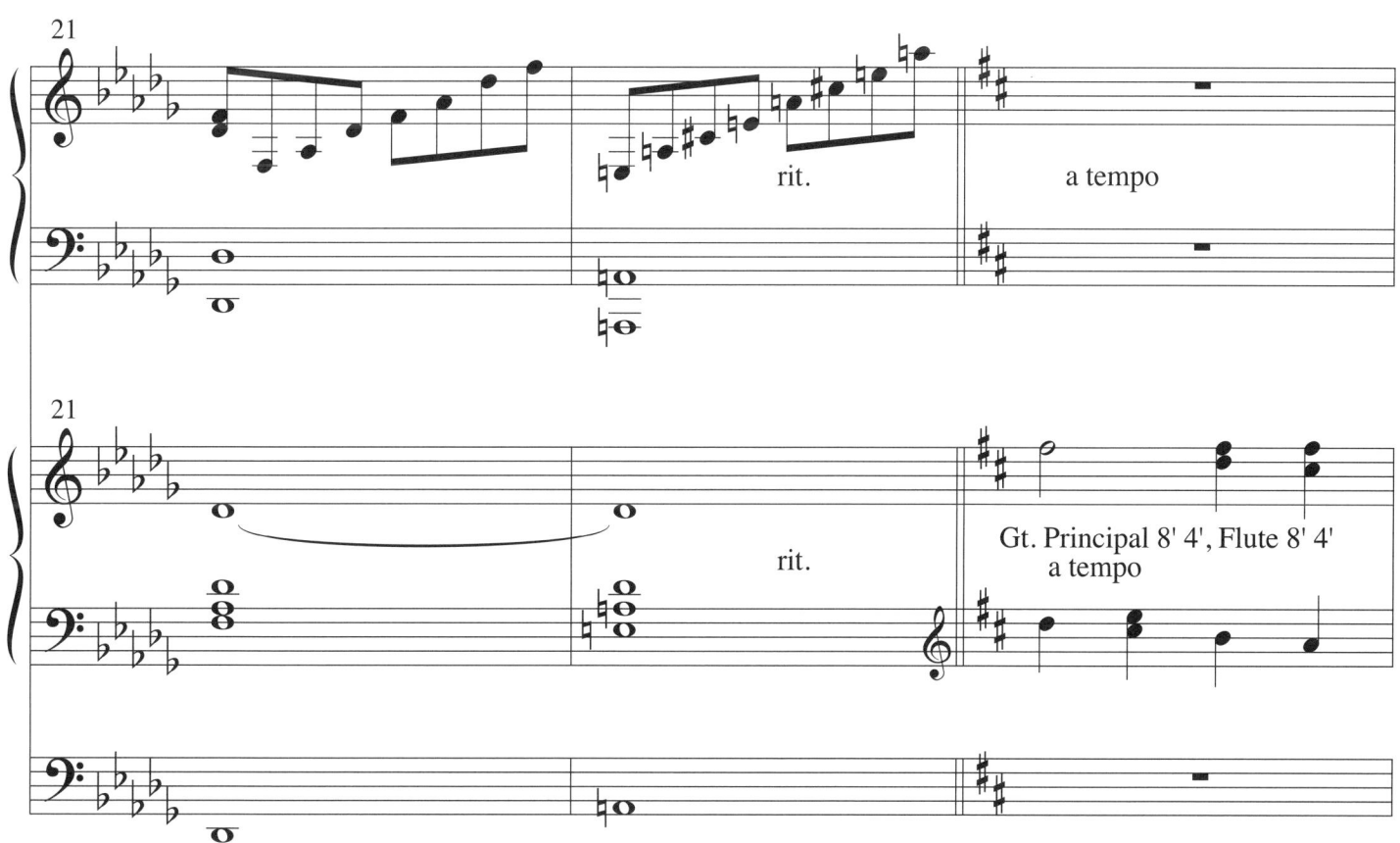

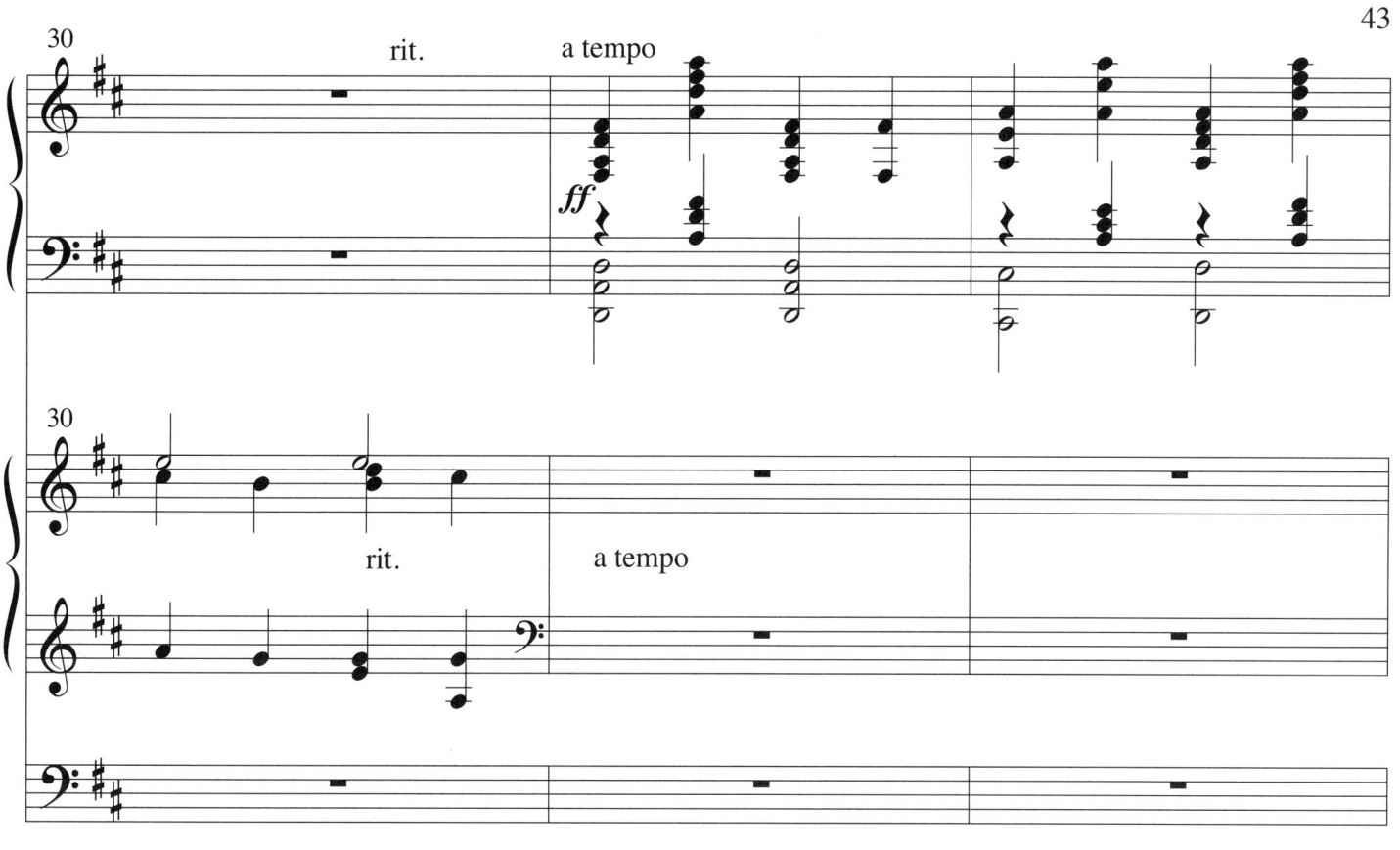

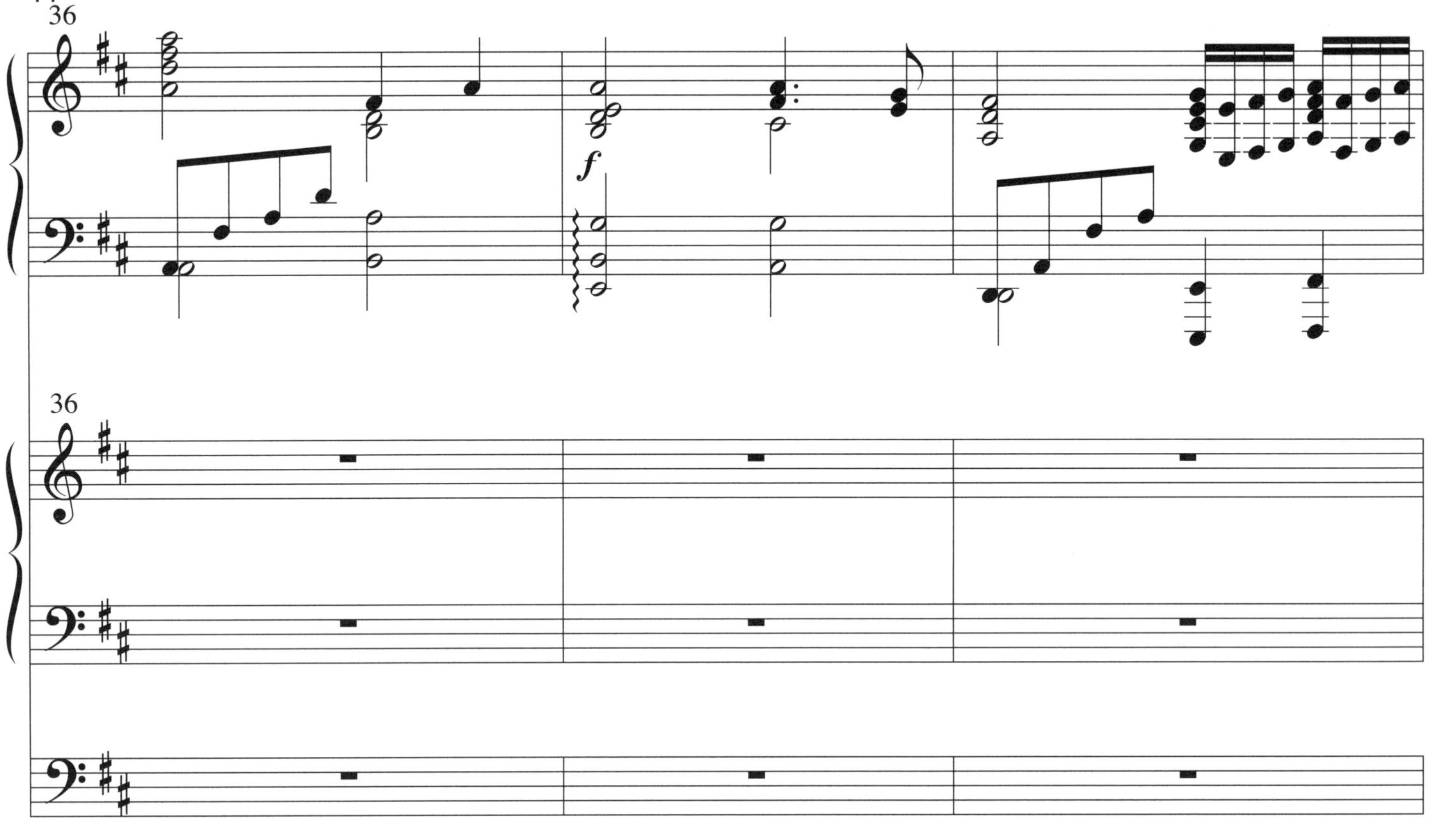
36
36

39
39
f +Diap. 2', Flute 2', trem.
+Bourden

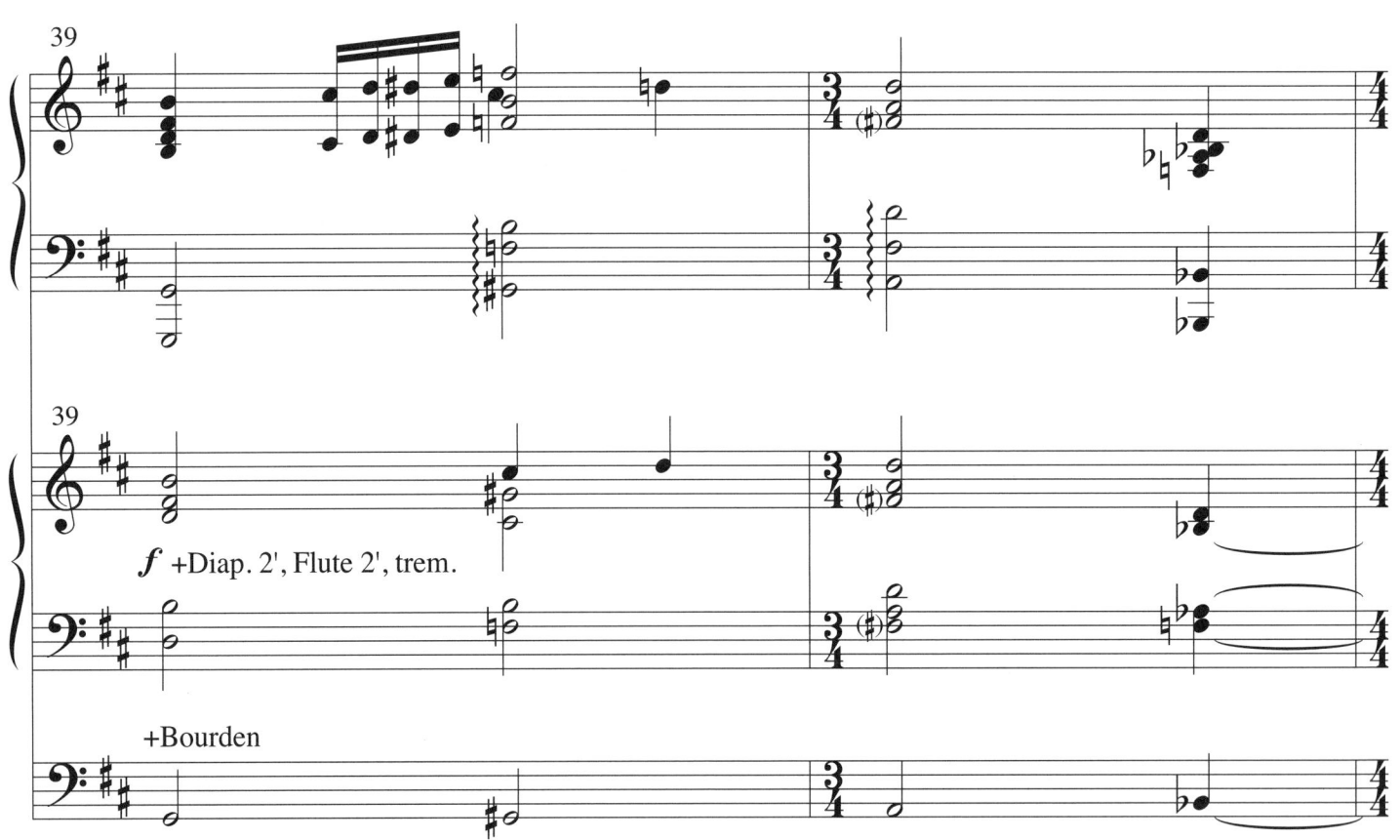

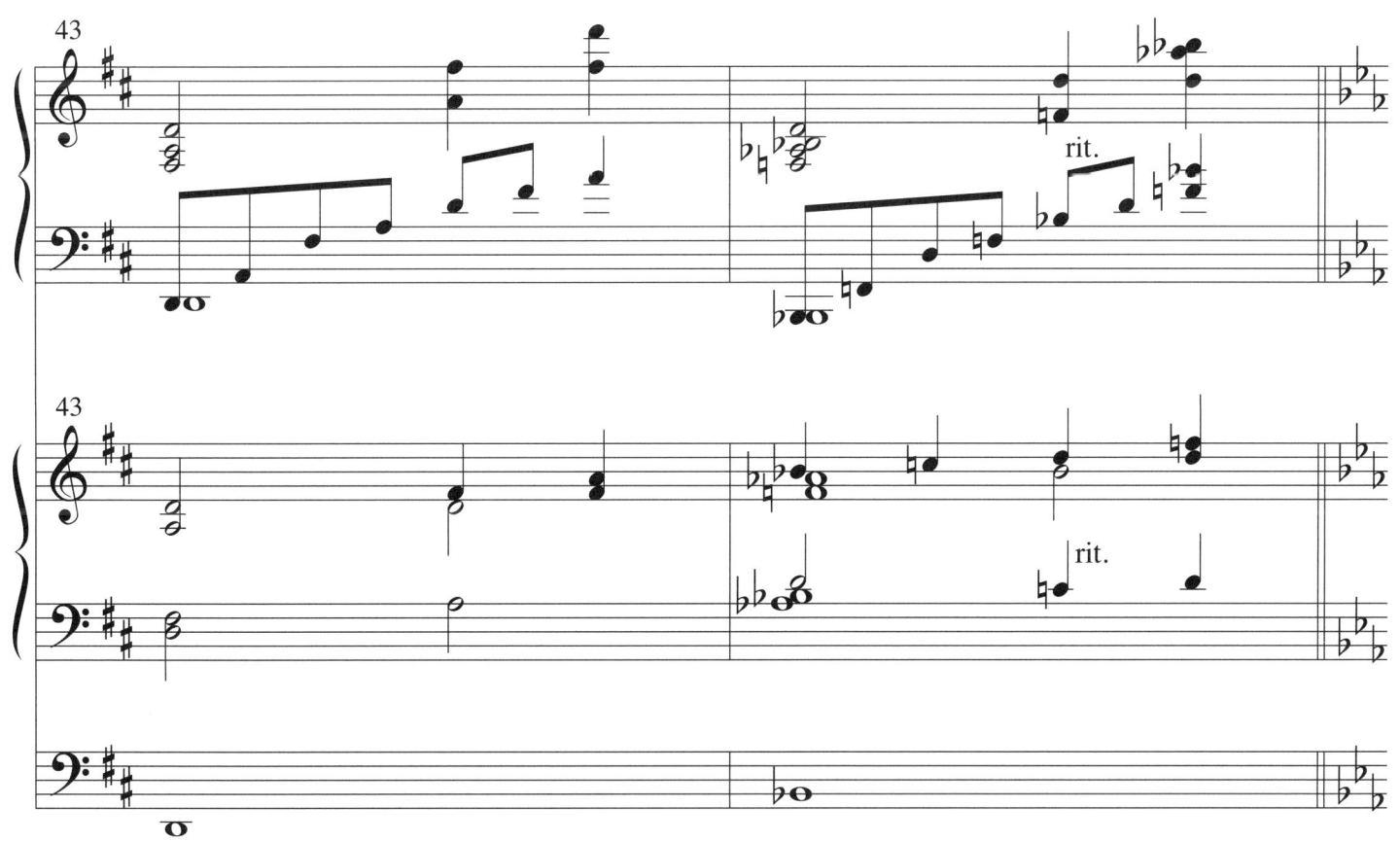

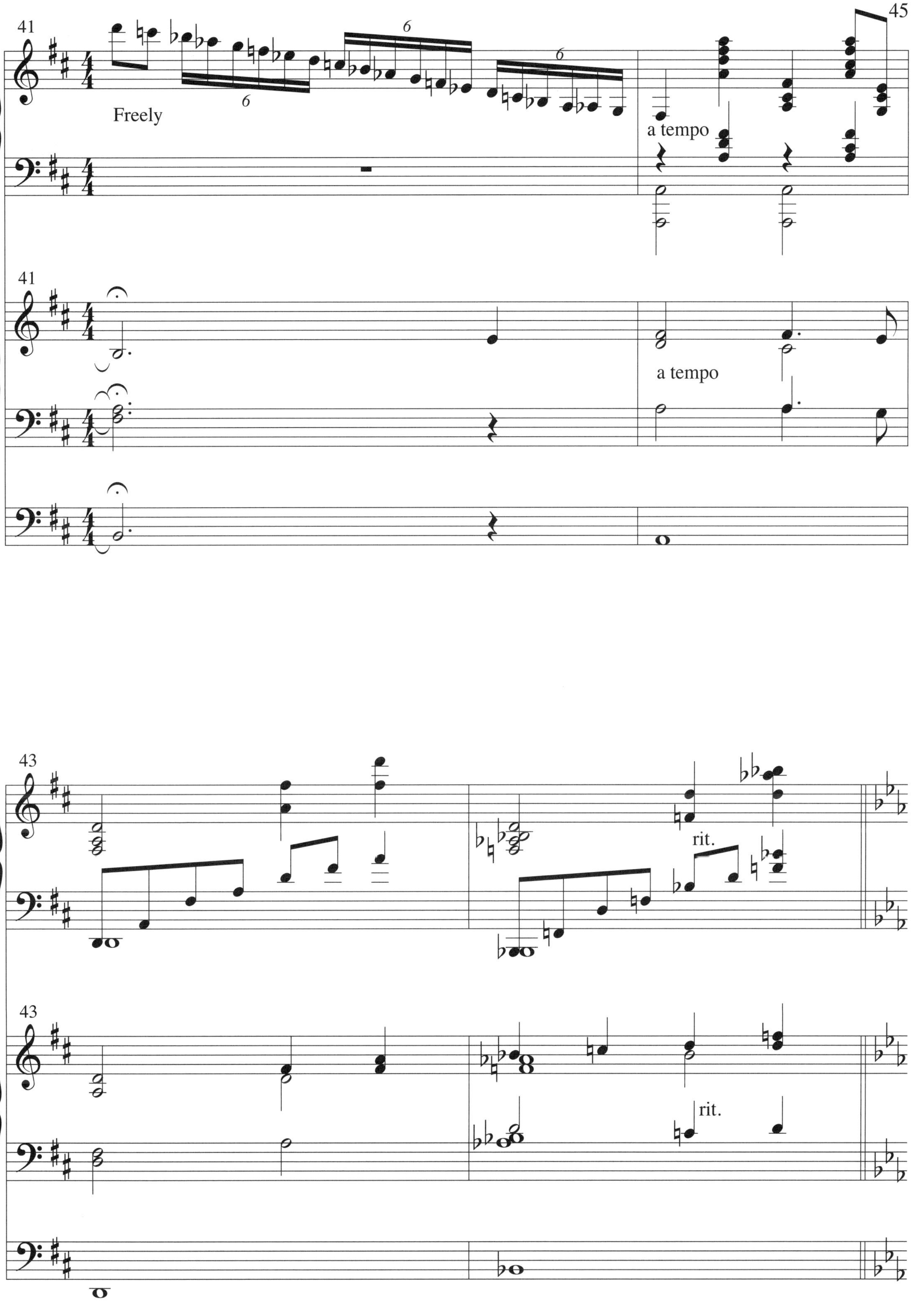
41
Freely
6
6
a tempo
41
a tempo
43
rit.
43
rit.

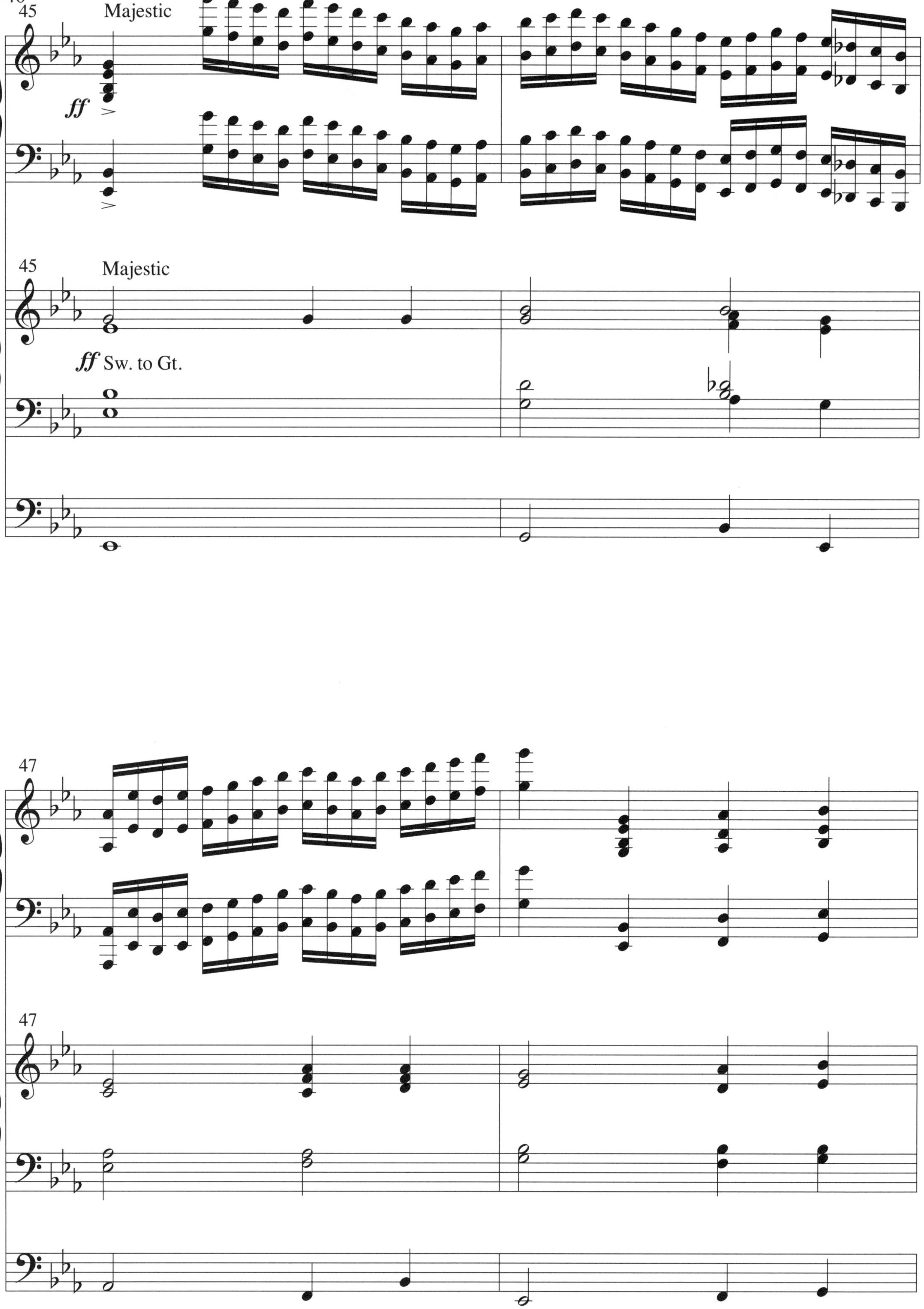
45
Majestic
ff
45
Majestic
ff Sw. to Gt.
47
47

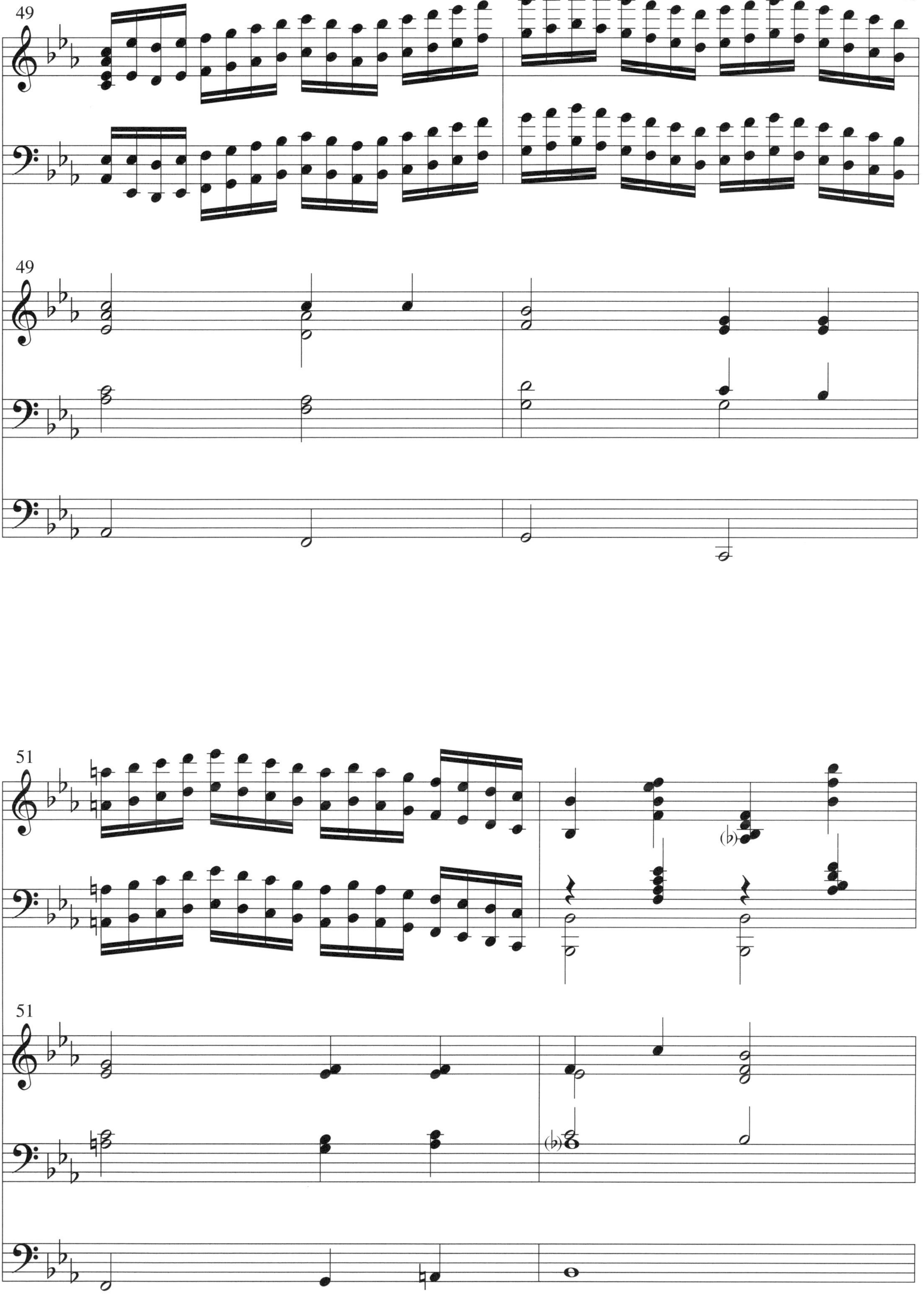
49
49
51
51

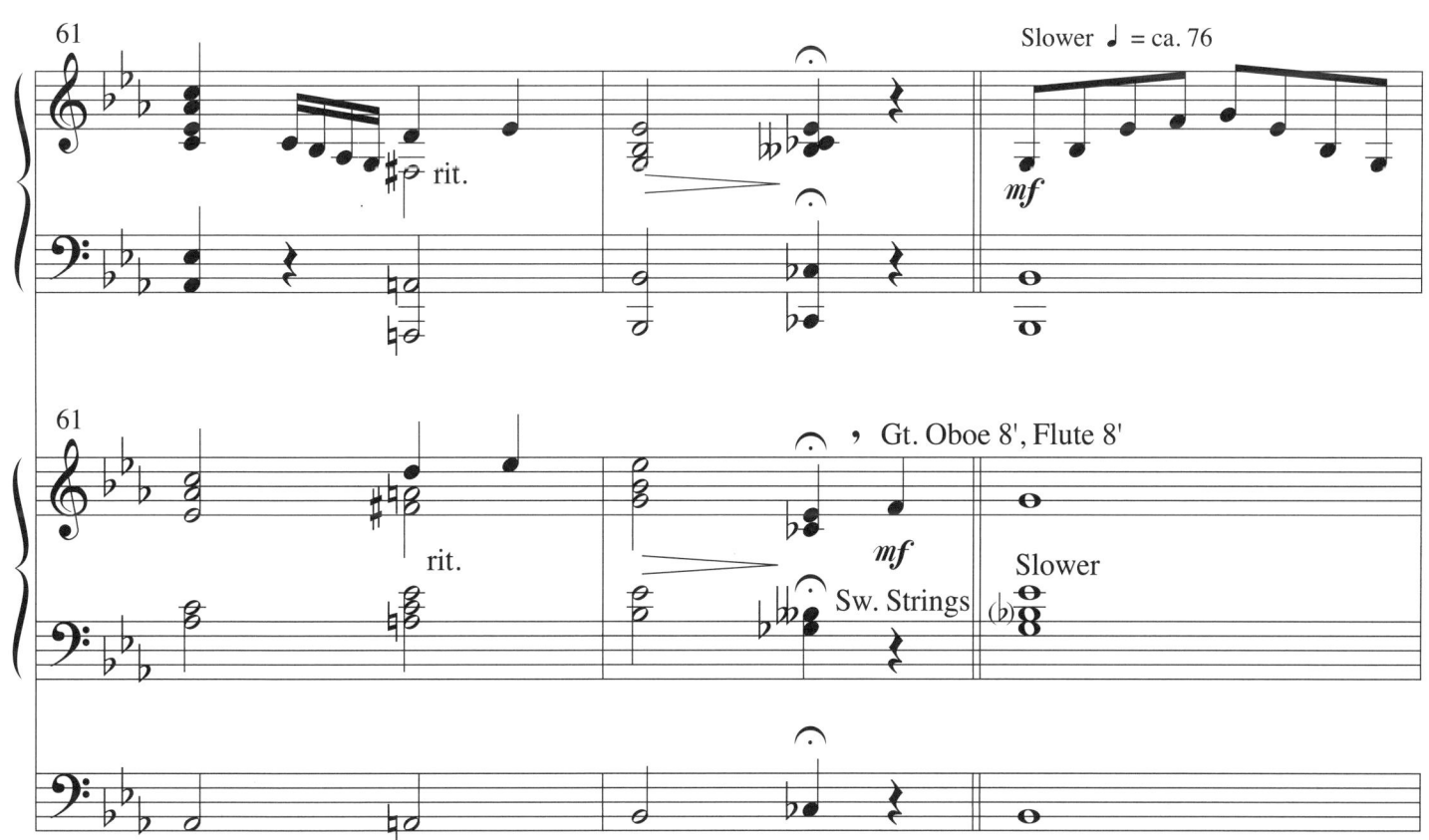

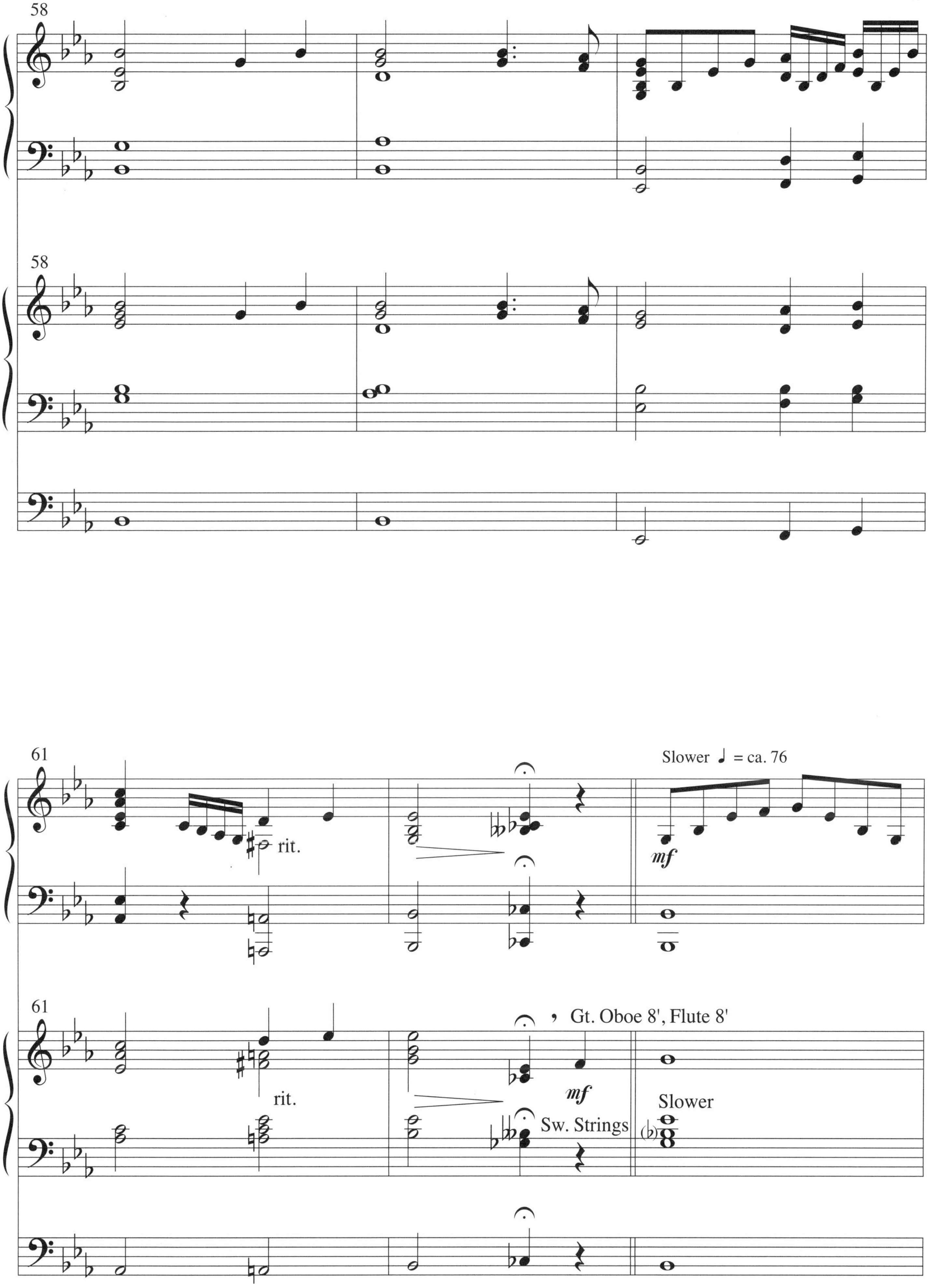
58
58
61
rit.
Slower ♩ = ca. 76
mf
61
Gt. Oboe 8', Flute 8'
rit.
mf
Sw. Strings
Slower

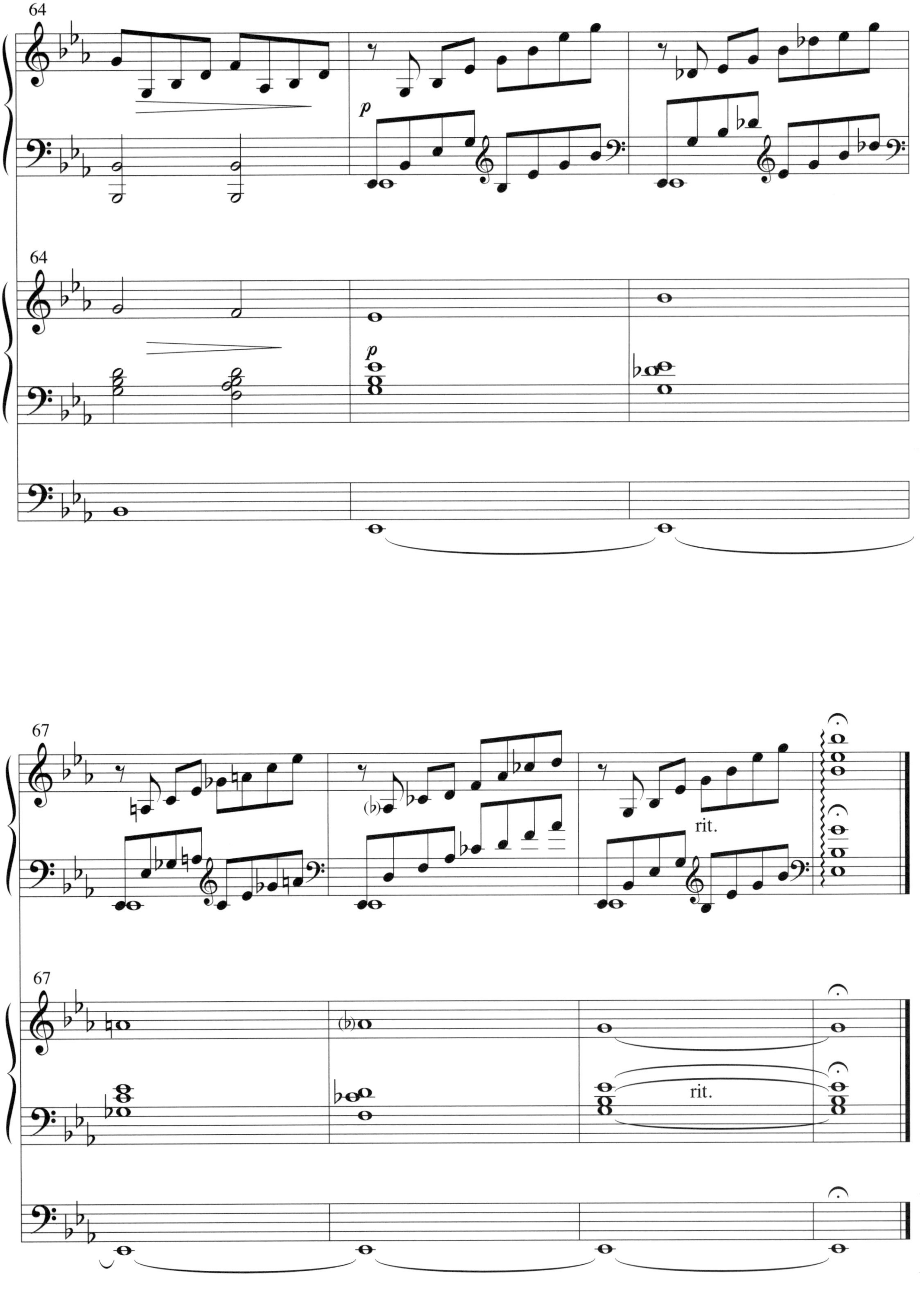
64
p
64
p
67
rit.
67
rit.

Turn Your Eyes upon Jesus

Sw. Strings 8' 4' 2', Trem.
Gt.   Dulce 8', Flute 8' 4', Trem.
Ped. Bourdon 16', Flute 8'

HELEN H. LEMMEL
Arranged by Paul Ferrin

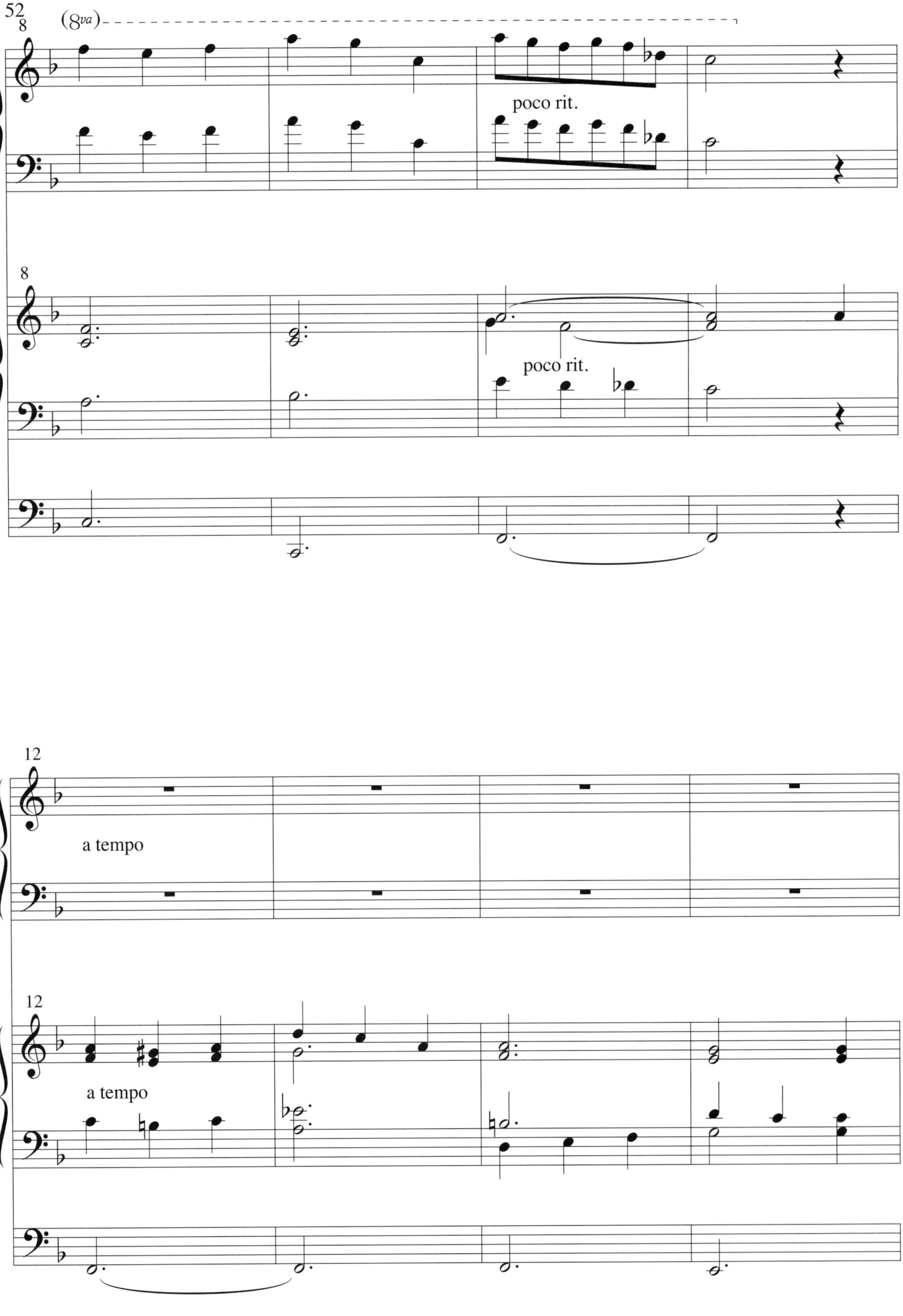
8
(8va)
poco rit.
8
poco rit.
12
a tempo
12
a tempo

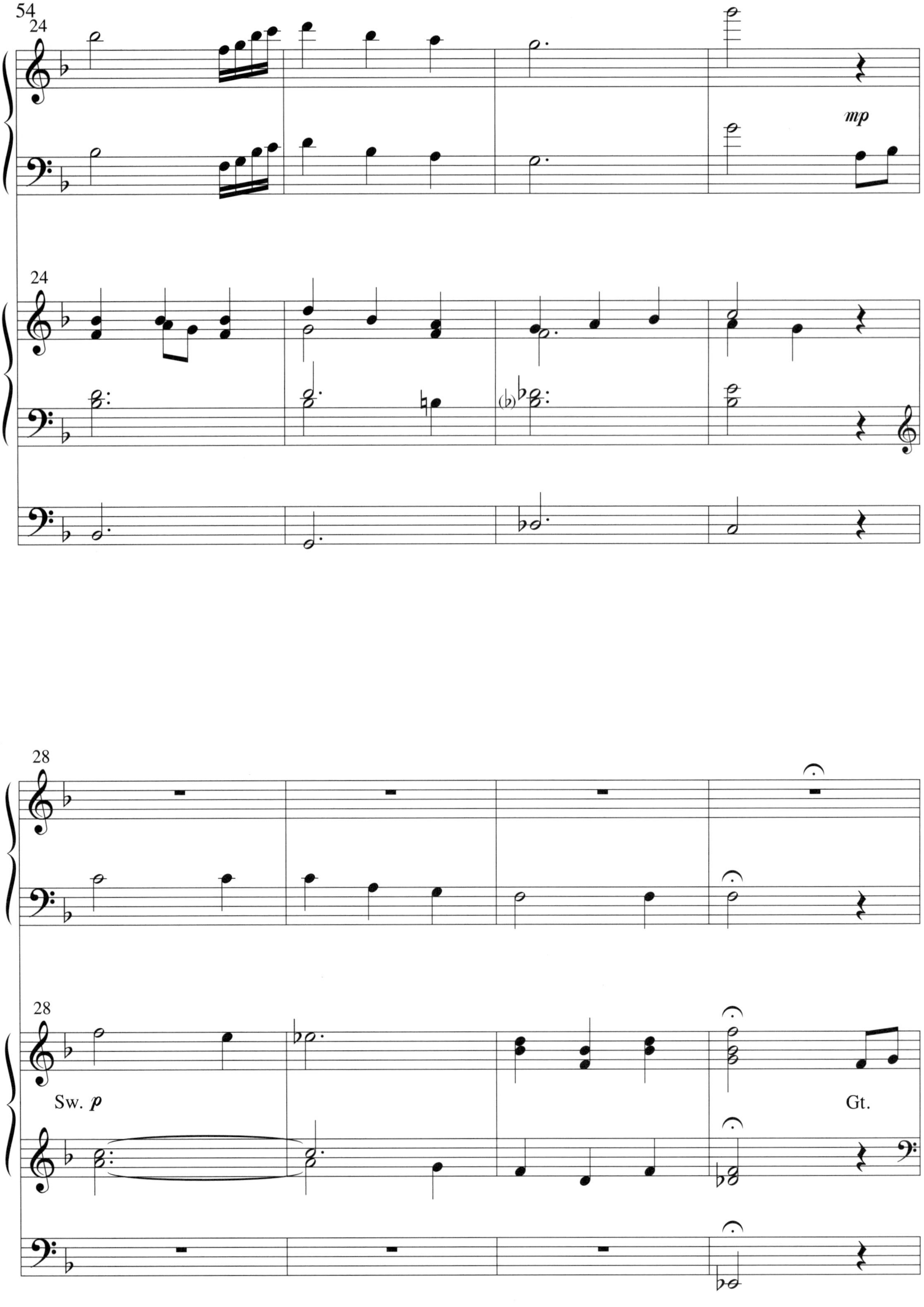
24
mp
24
(♭)
28
28
Sw. p
Gt.

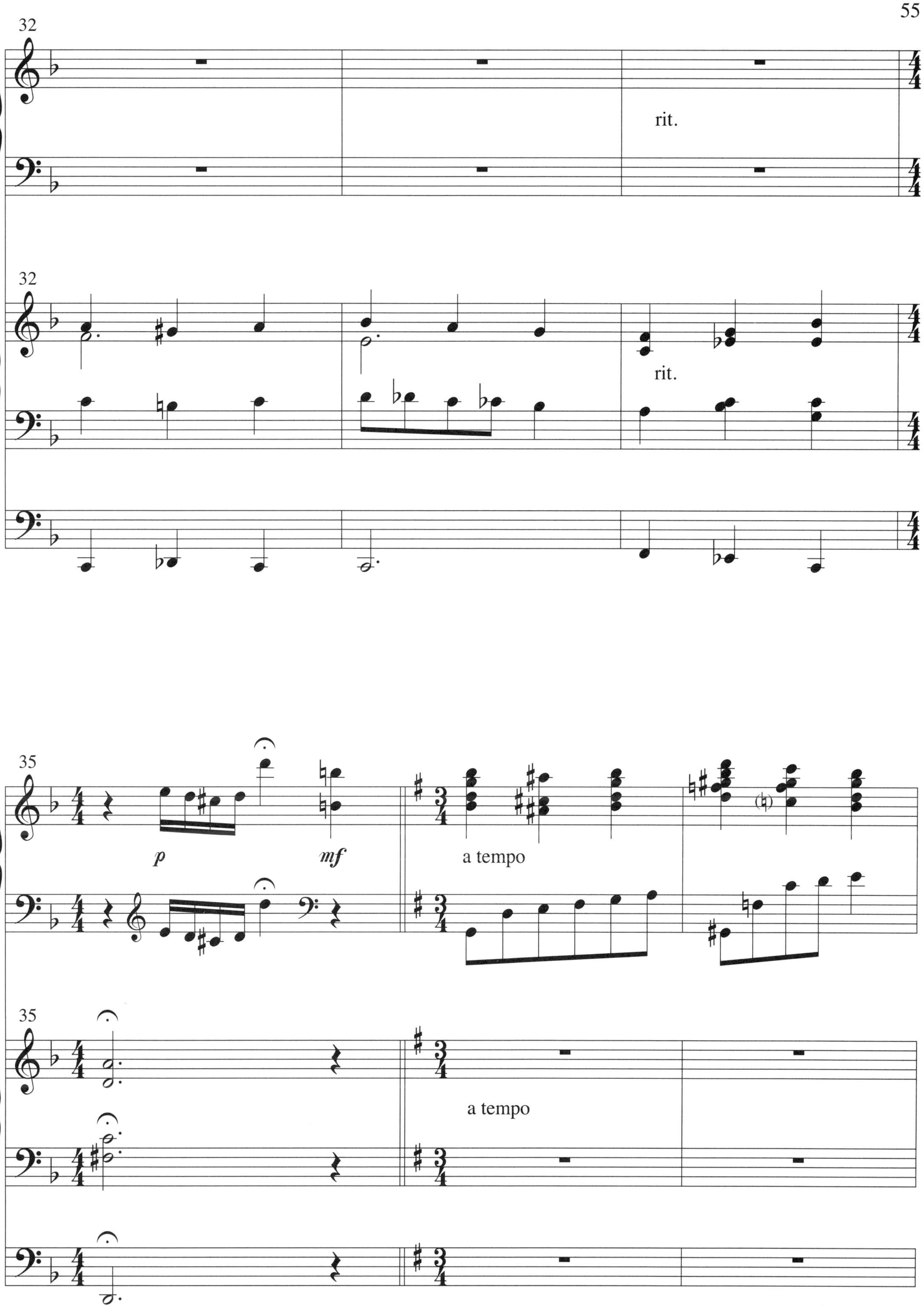
32
rit.
32
rit.
35
p
mf
a tempo
35
a tempo

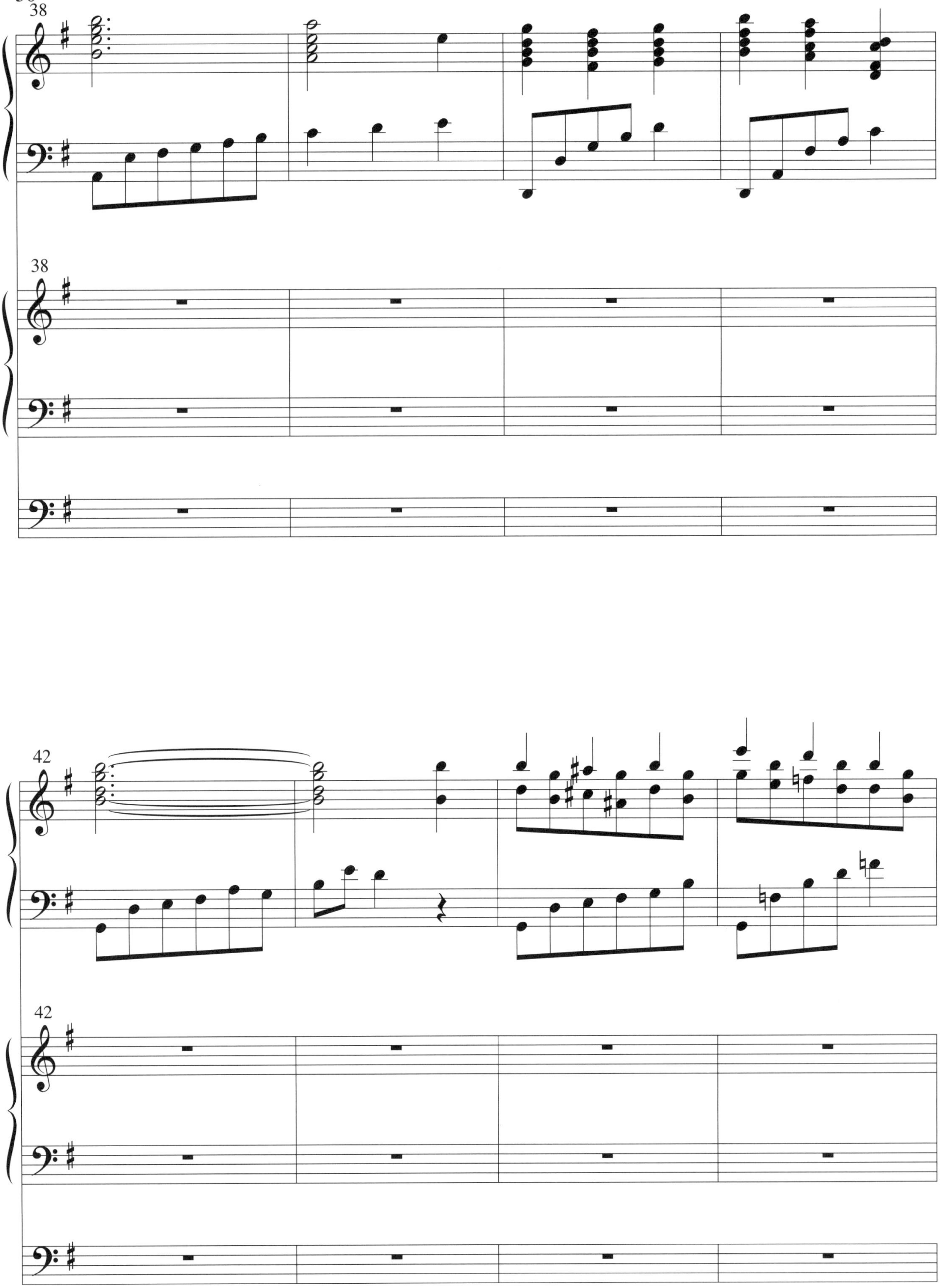
38
38
42
42

46
46

50
cresc.
rit.
f a tempo
Full Organ
50
Gt. mf
cresc.
rit.
f a tempo

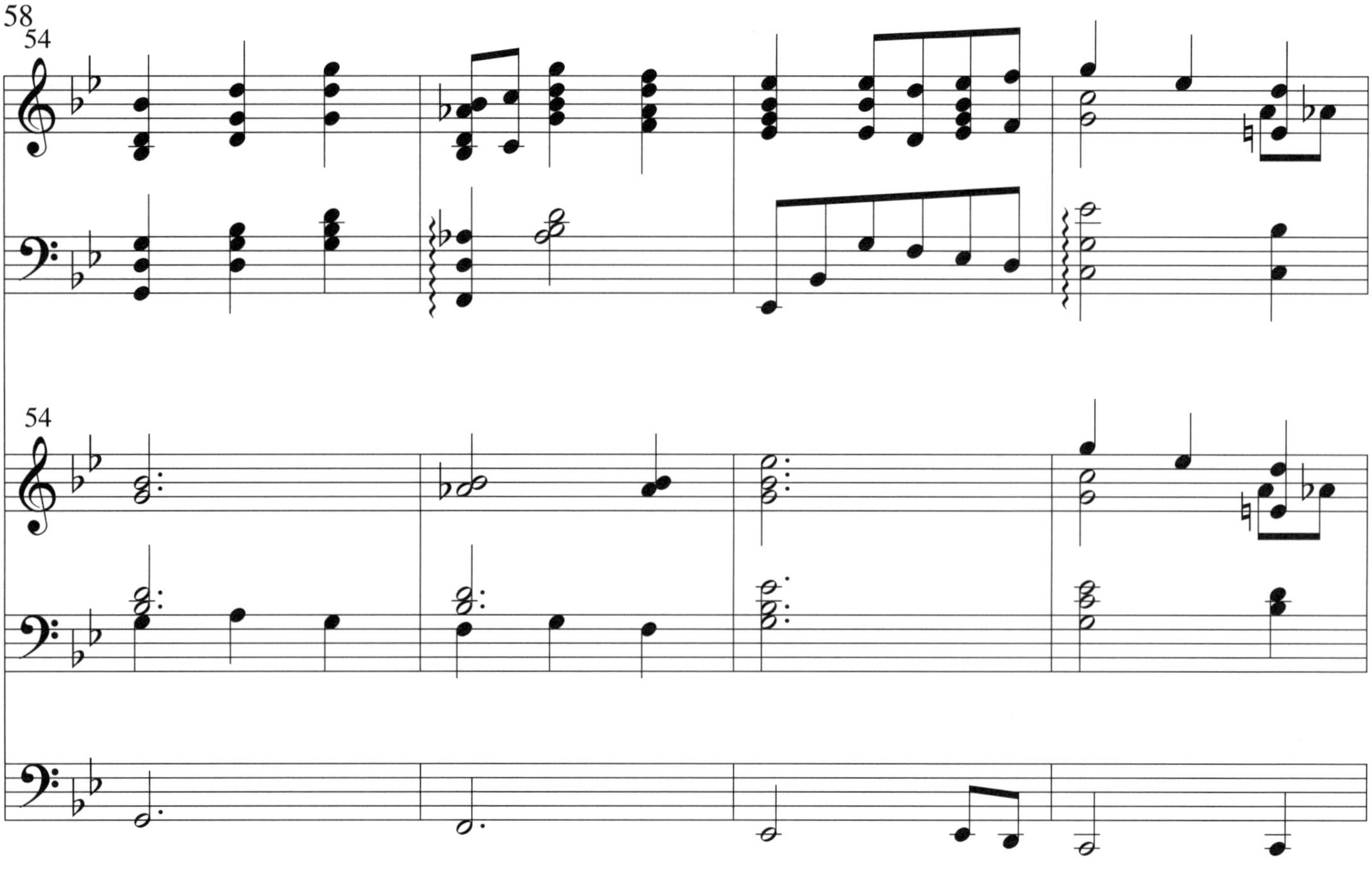
54
54

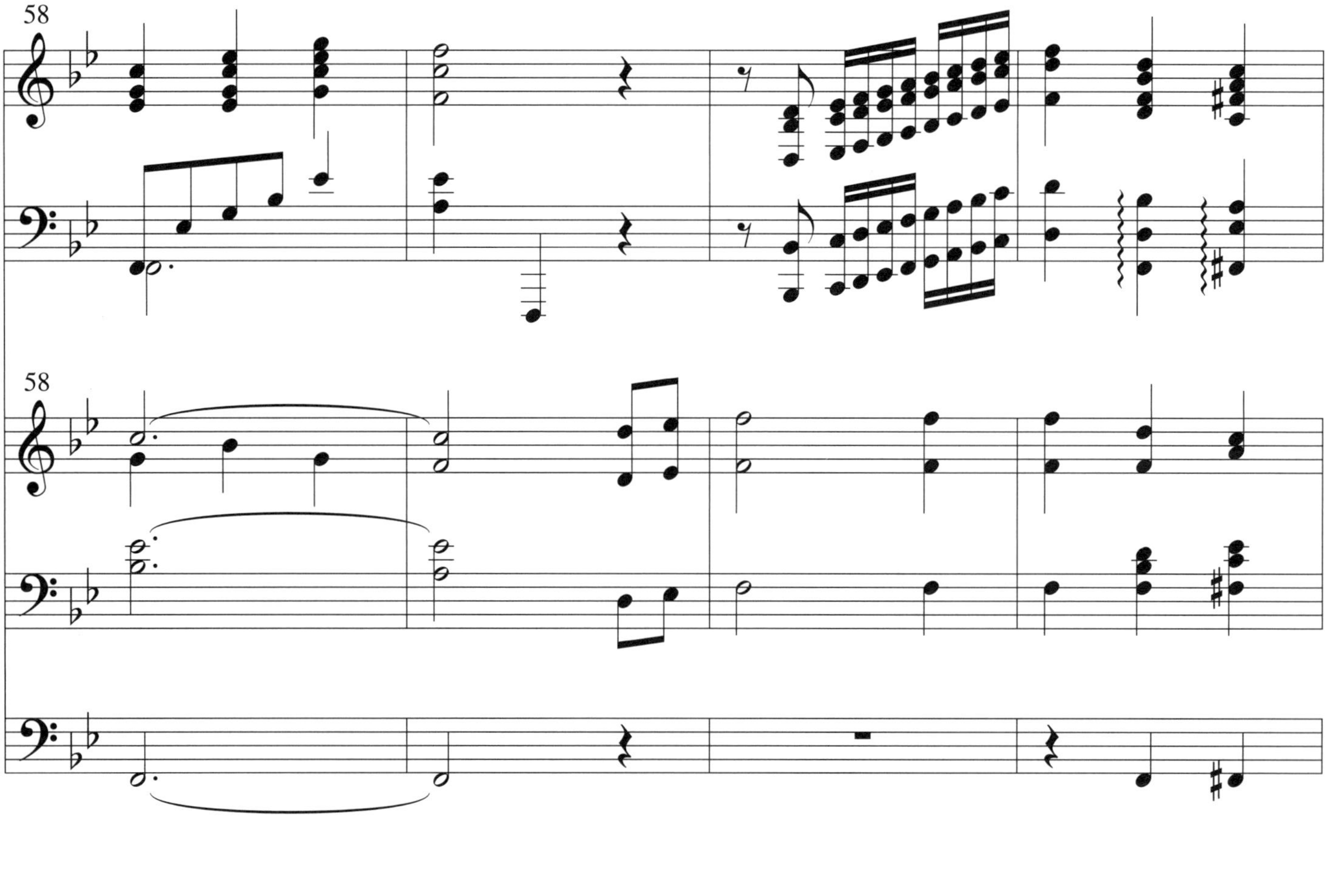
58
58

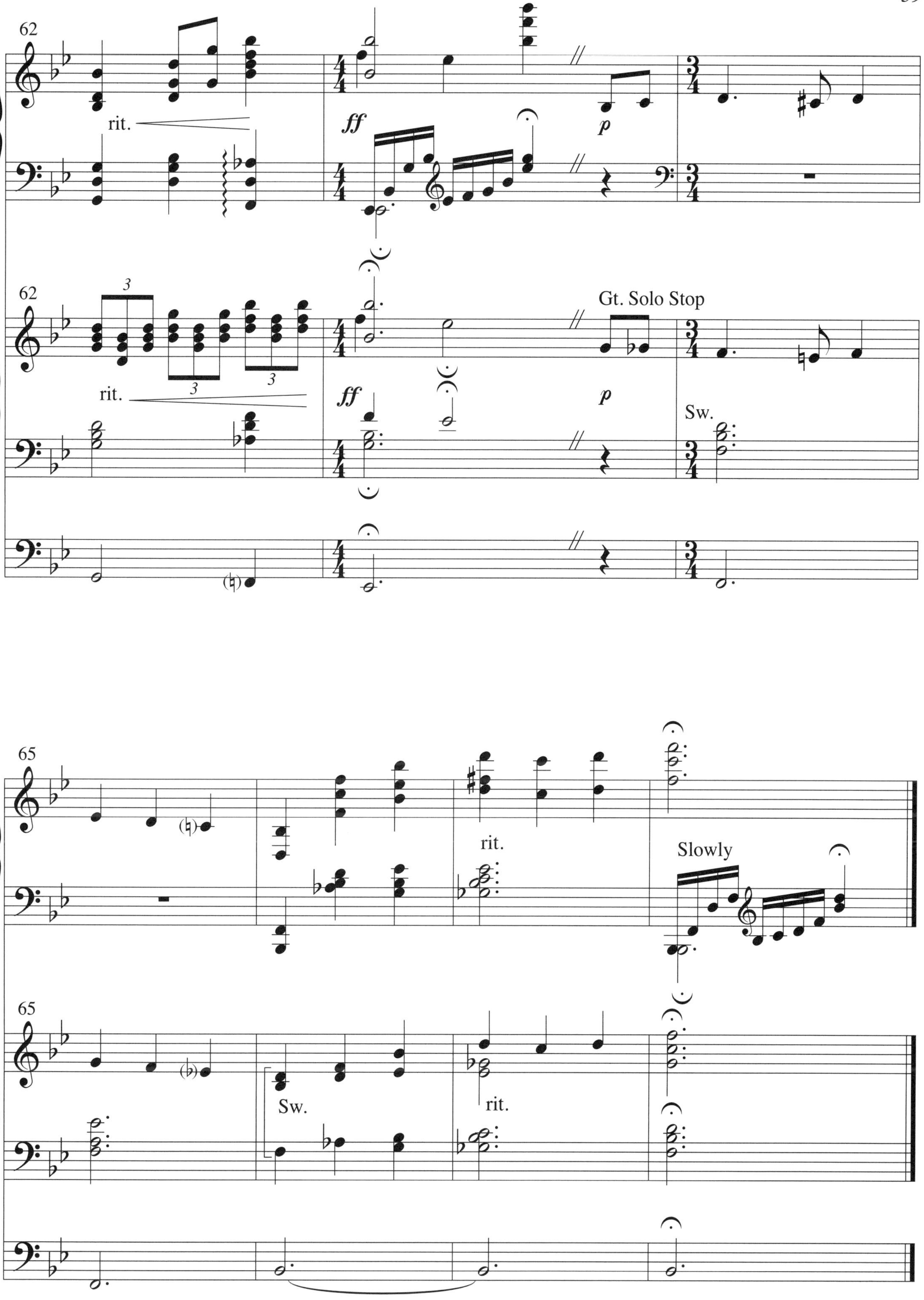
62
rit.
ff
p
62
rit.
ff
Gt. Solo Stop
p
Sw.
65
rit.
Slowly
65
Sw.
rit.

Like a River

Like a River Glorious
Peace like a River

Sw. Flute 8'
Gt. Principal 8' 4' 2'
Ped. Solo stop

Arranged by Paul Ferrin

With dignity and joy ♩ = ca. 69

"Like a River Glorious" (James Mountain)

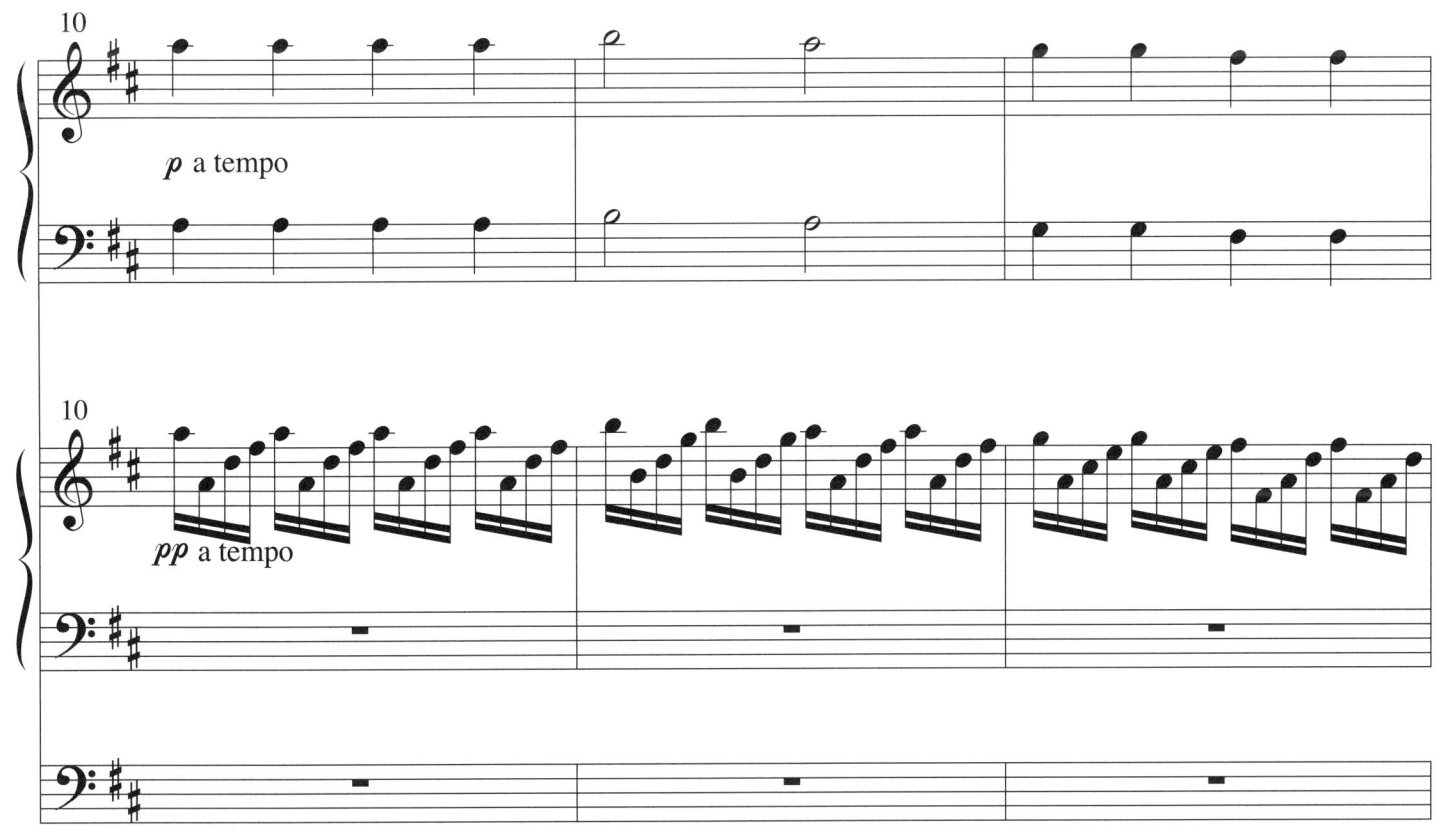

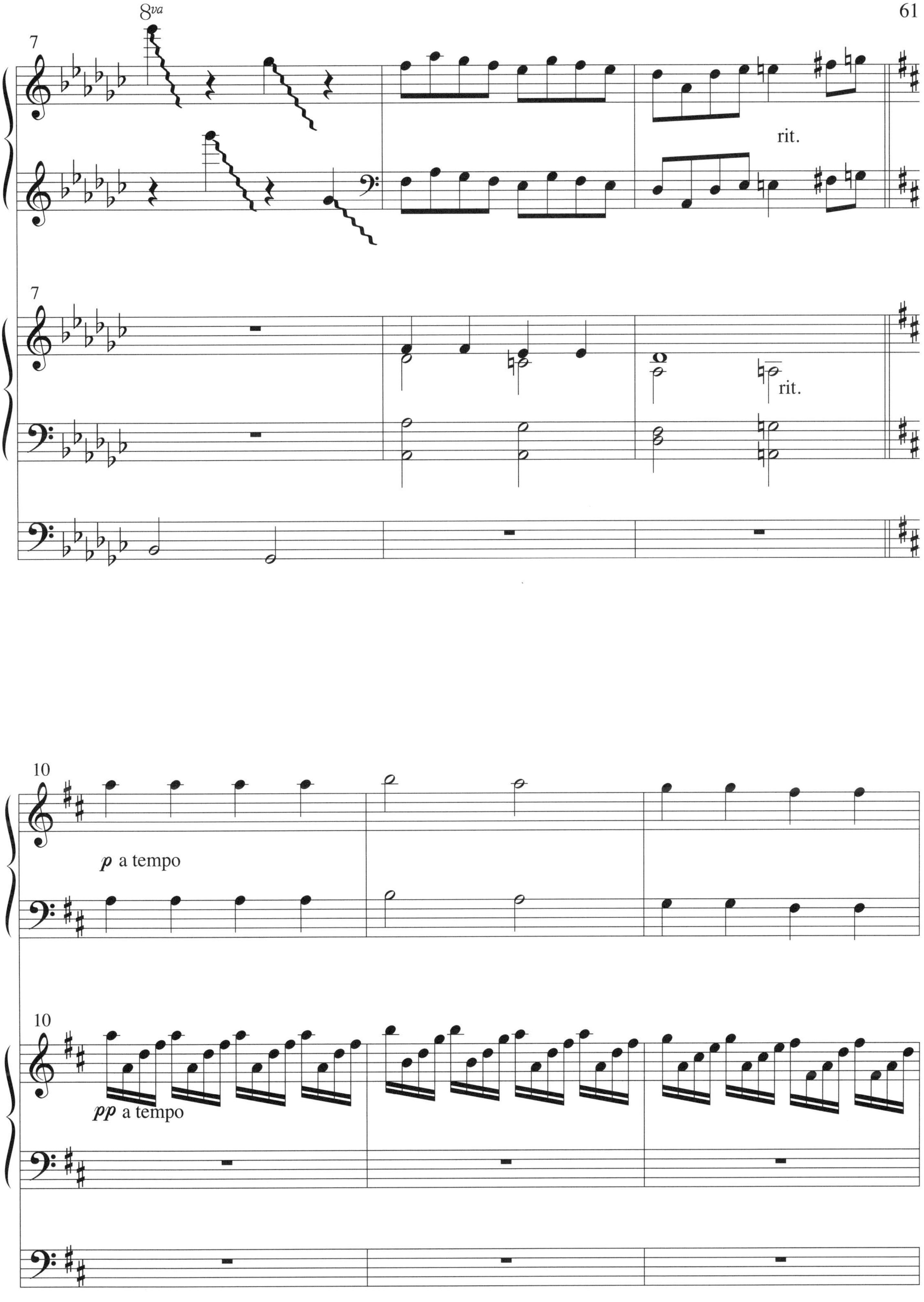
8va
7
rit.
7
rit.
10
p a tempo
10
pp a tempo

13
rit.
a tempo
Gt. + Flute 8' 4'
13
rit.
a tempo
16' 8'

16
rit.
a tempo
16
Sw. to Gt.
rit.
mf a tempo

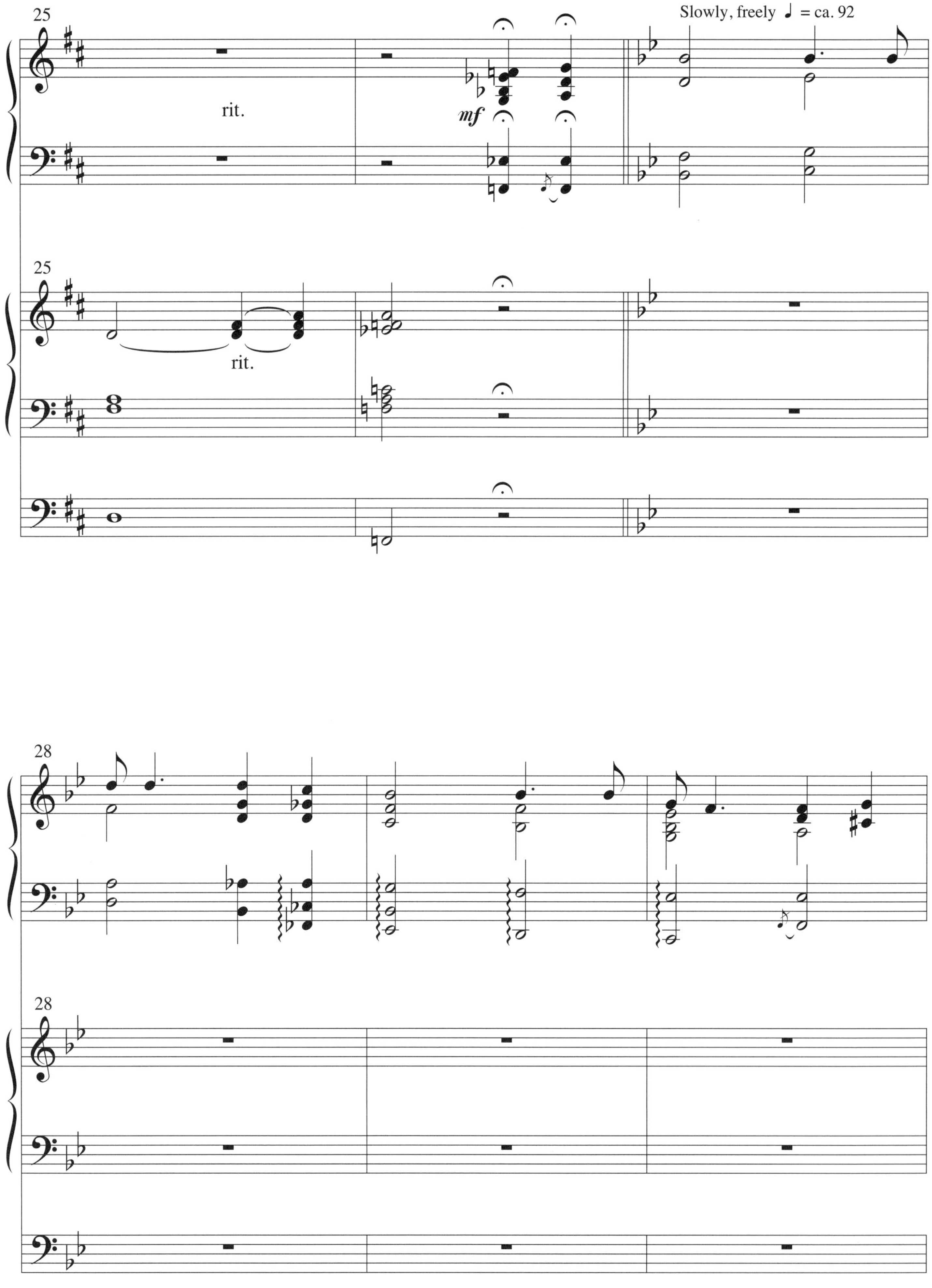

"Peace like a River" (Spiritual)

Slowly, freely ♩ = ca. 92

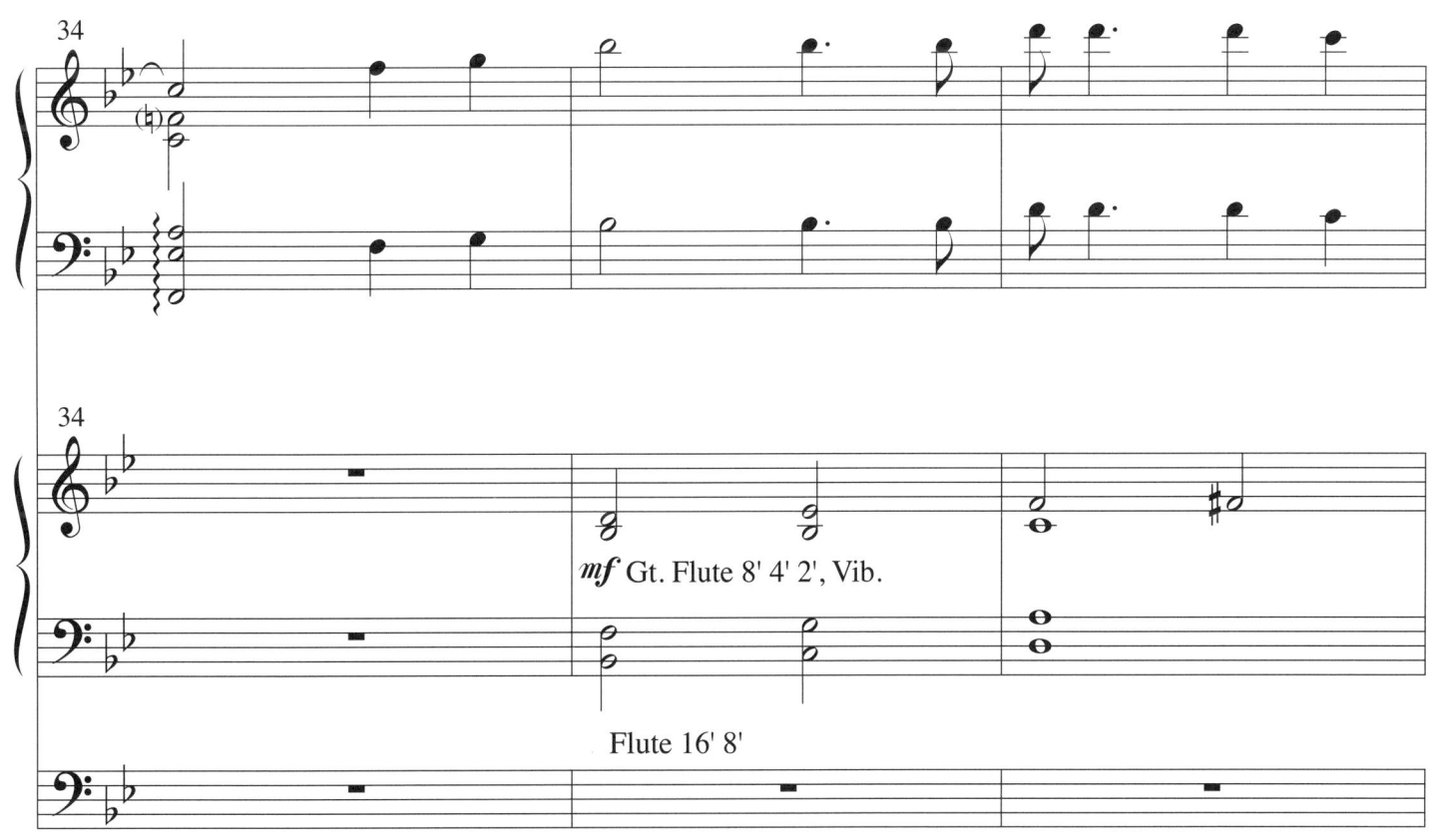

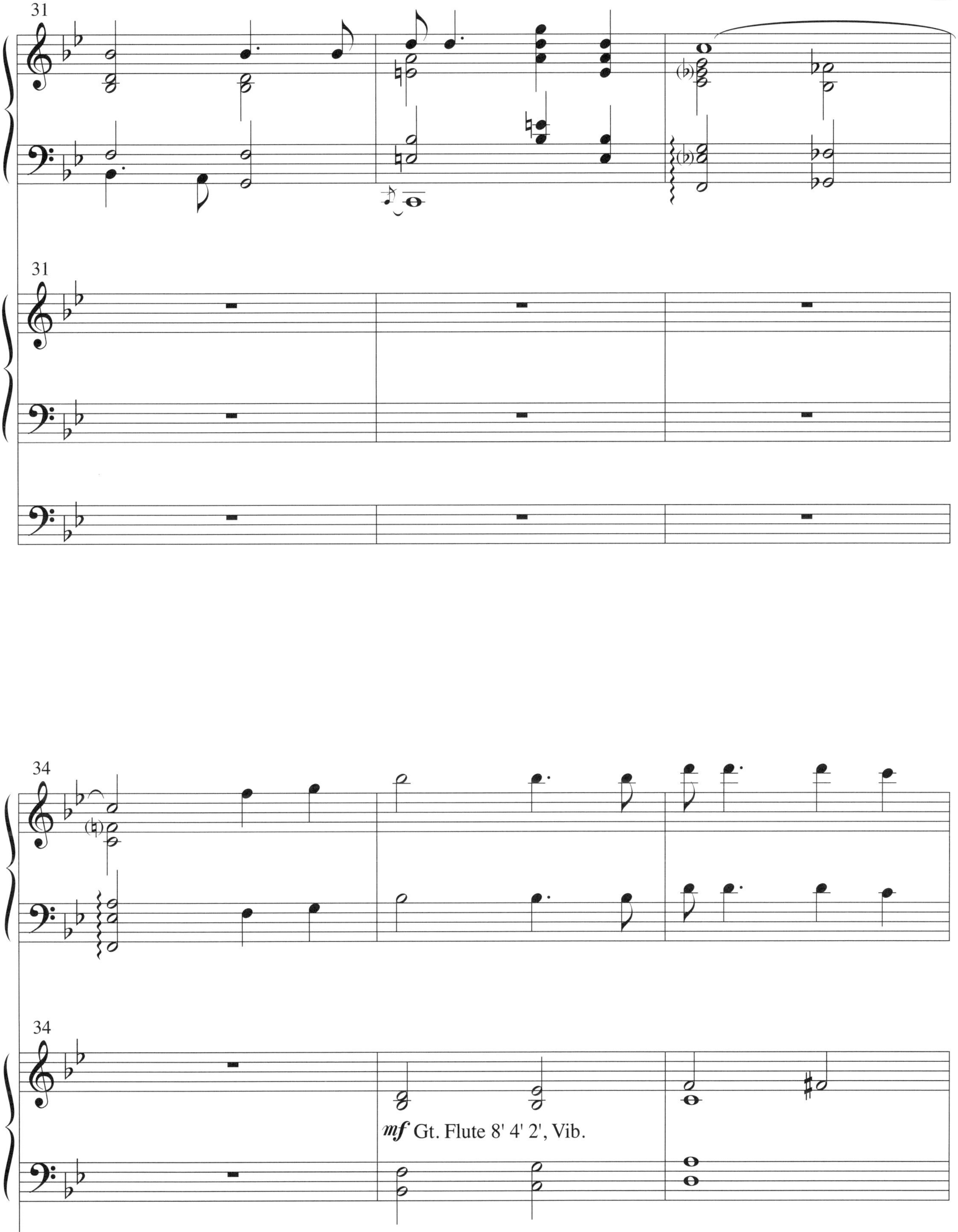
31
31
34
34
mf Gt. Flute 8' 4' 2', Vib.
Flute 16' 8'

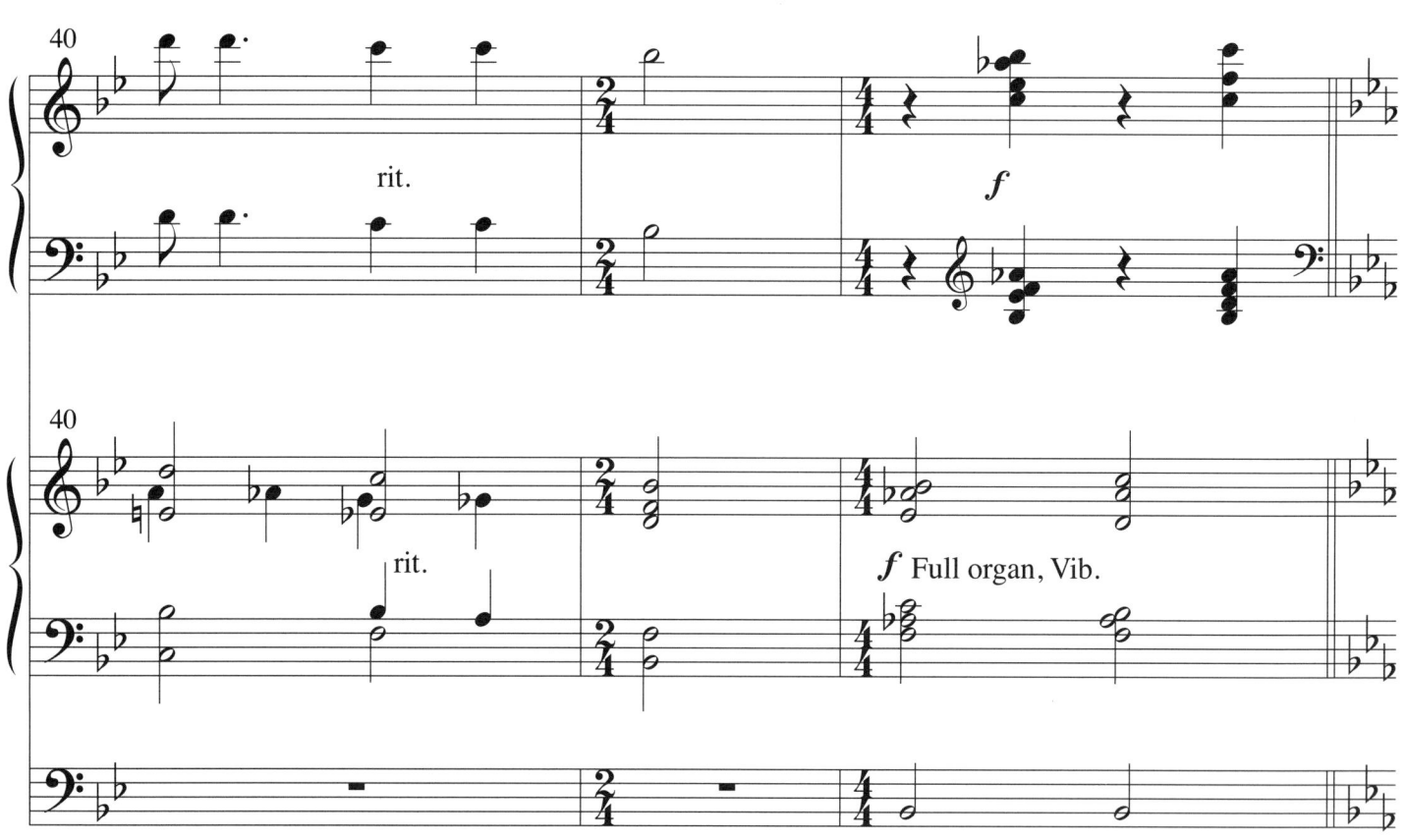

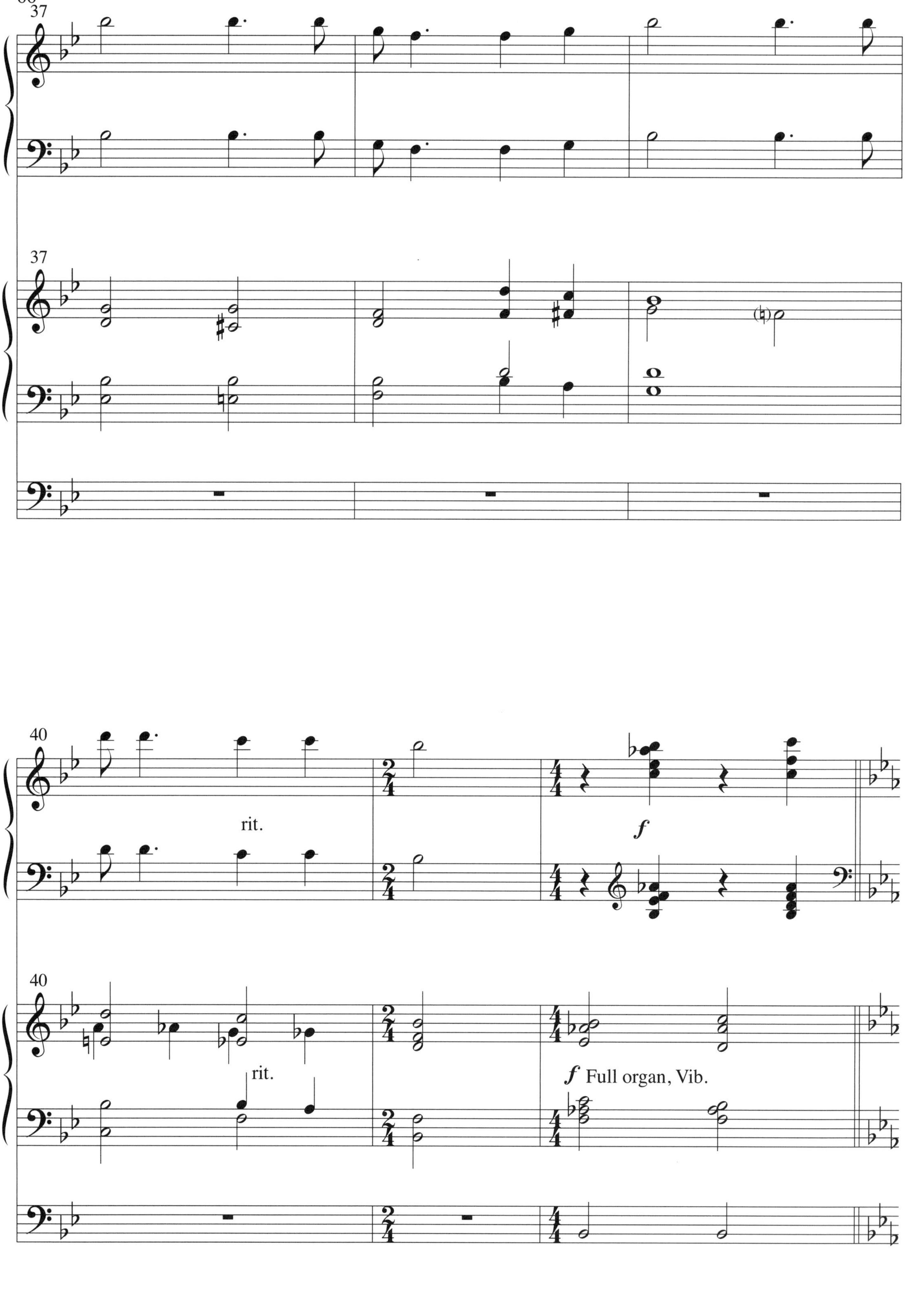
37
37
40
rit.
f
40
rit.
f Full organ, Vib.

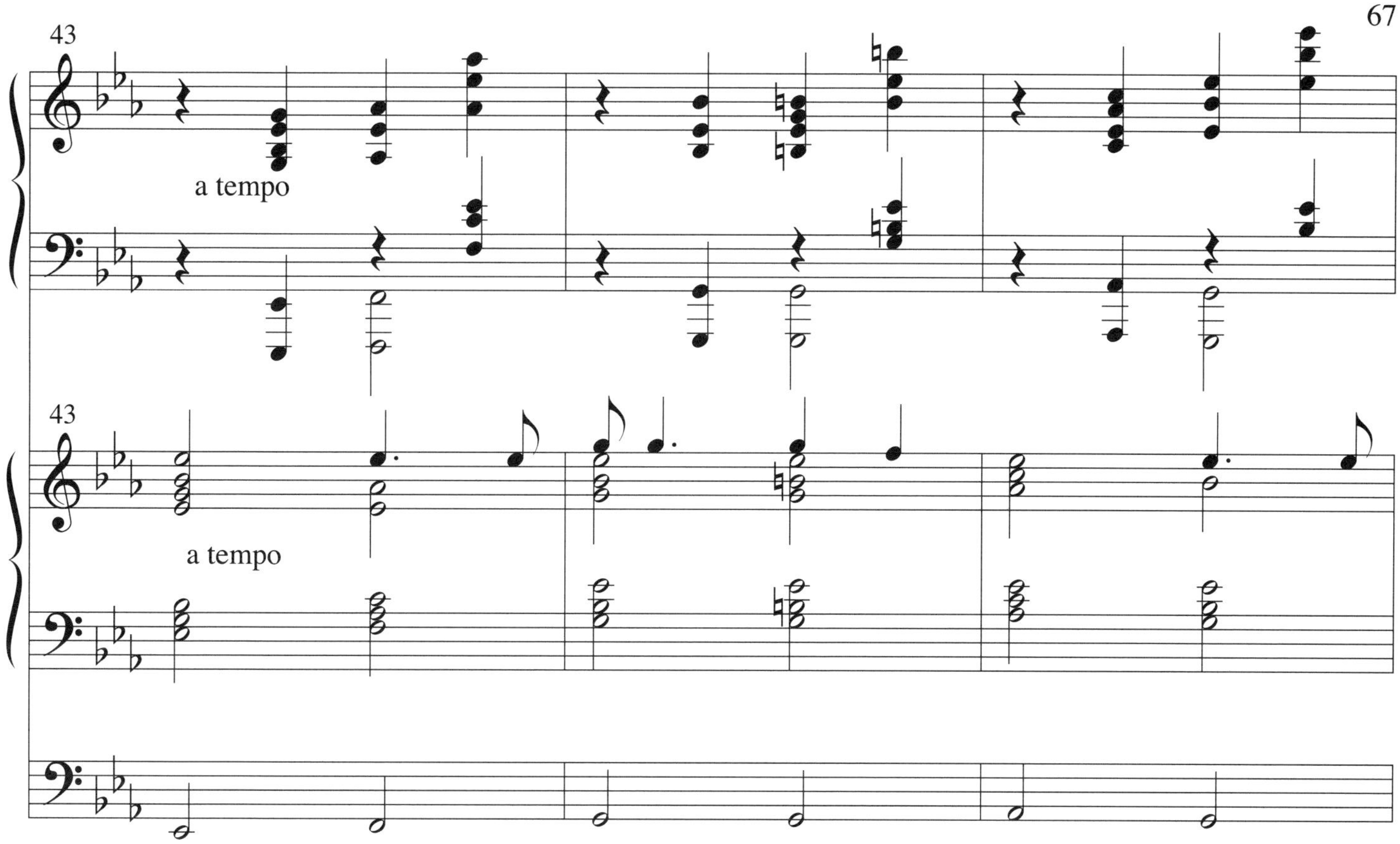
43
a tempo
43
a tempo

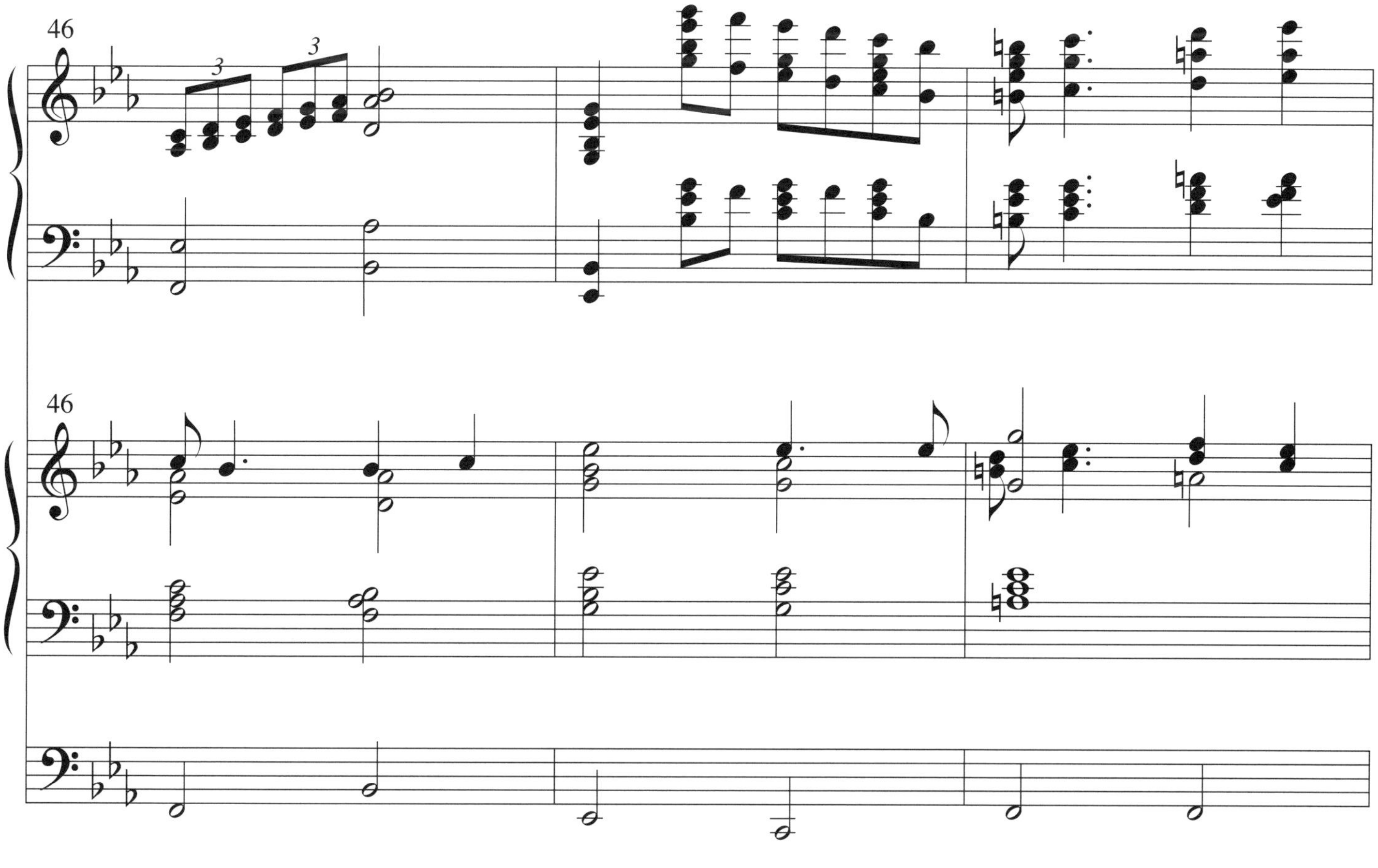
46
3
3
46

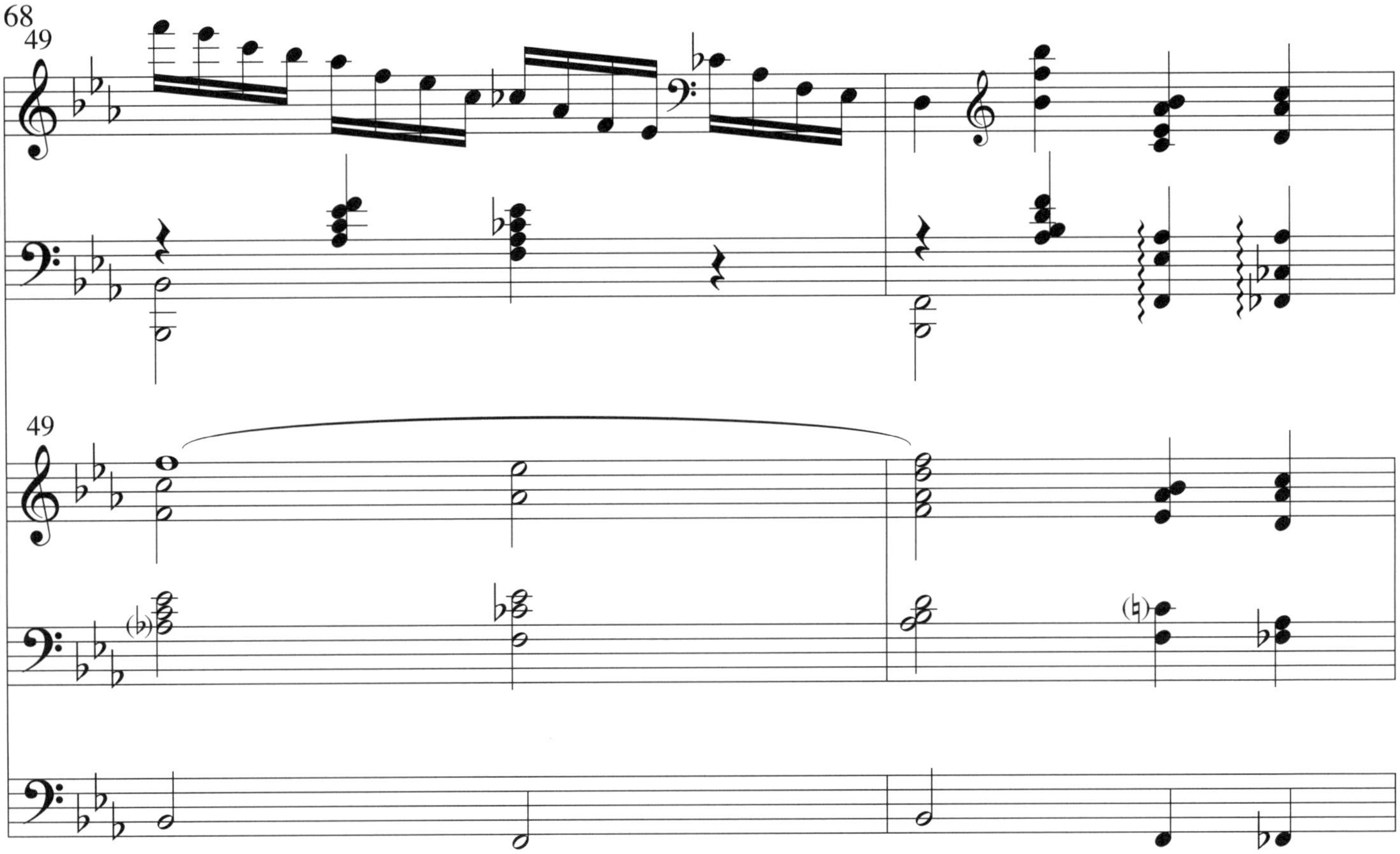
49
49

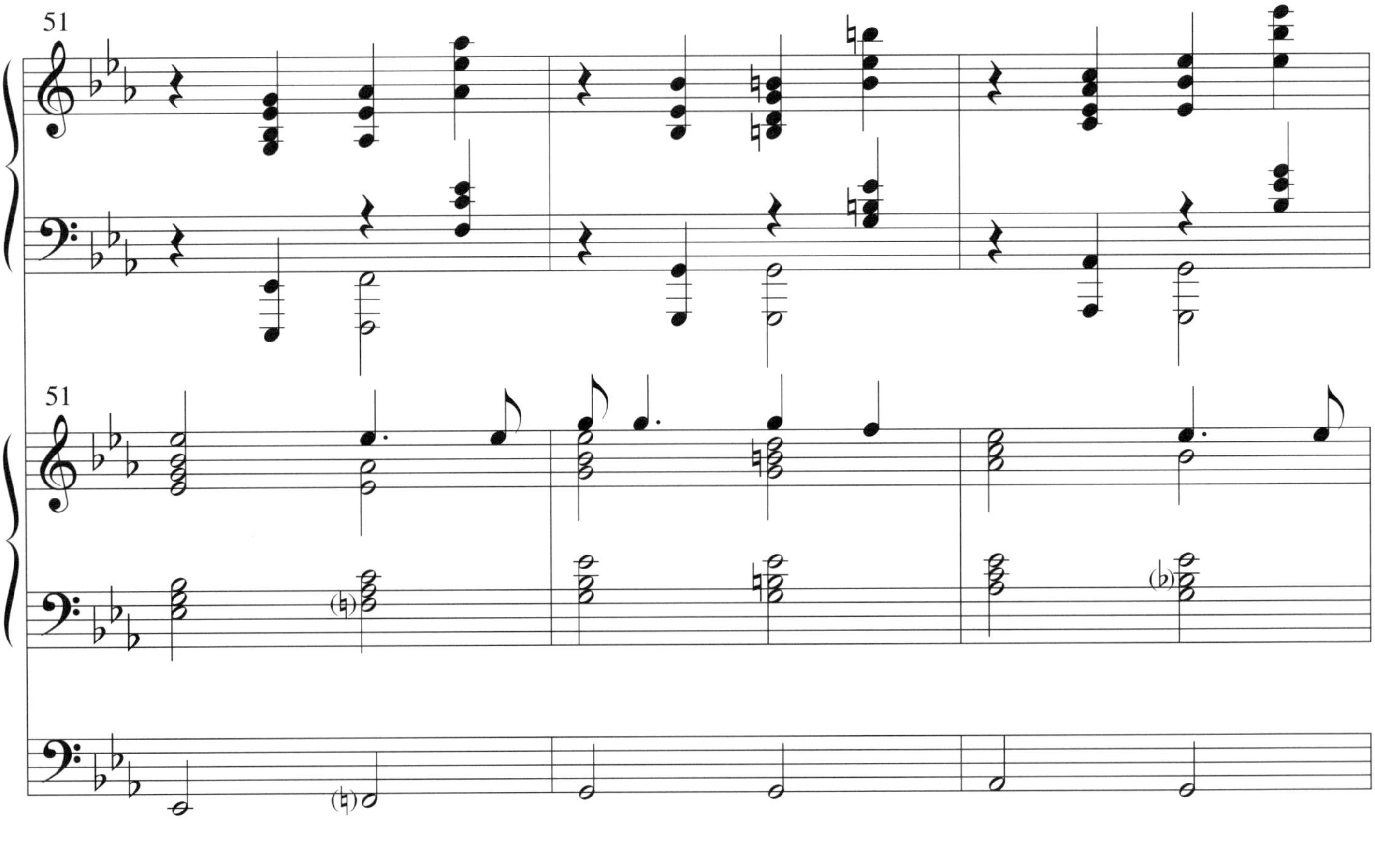
51
51

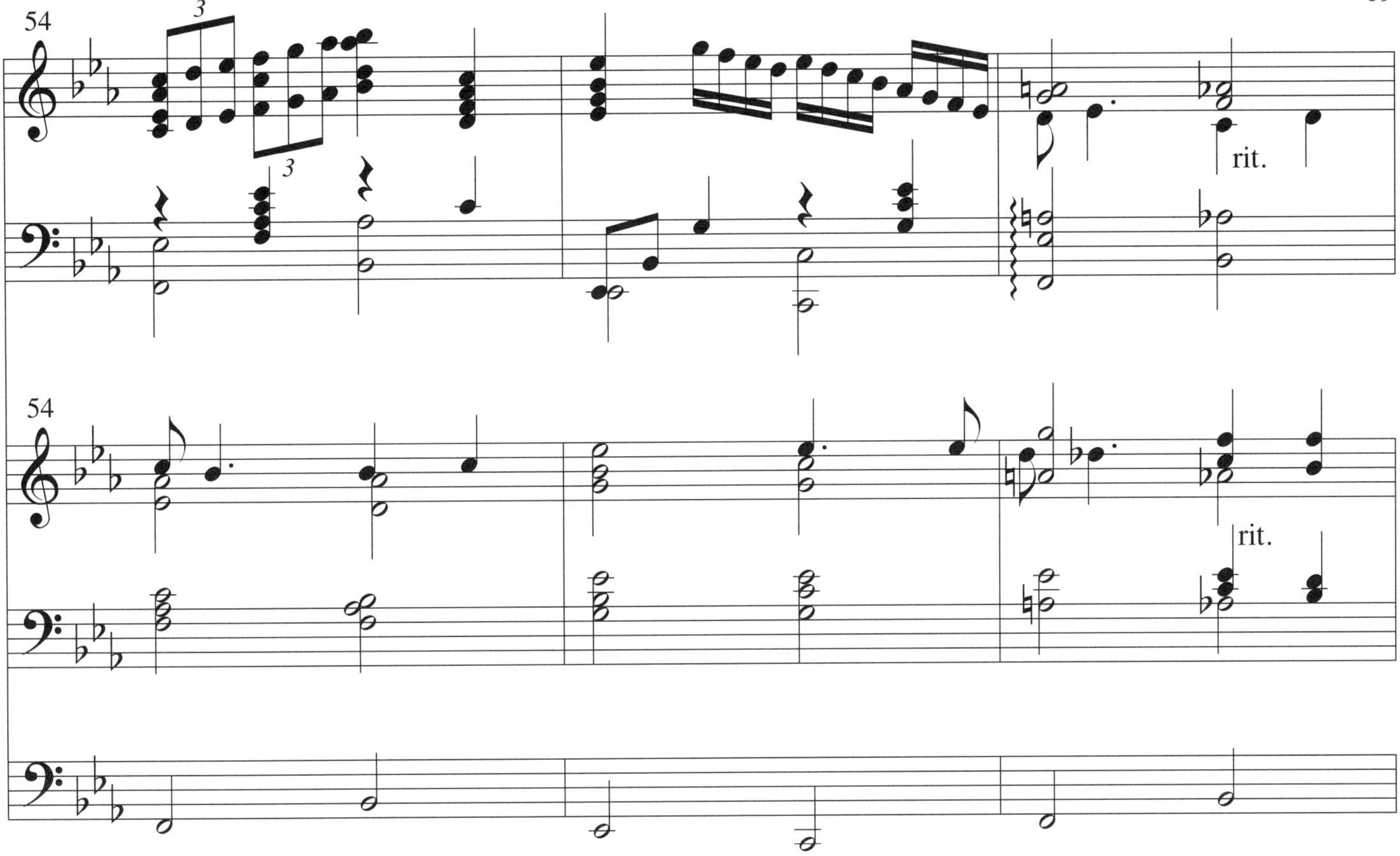
54
3
3
rit.
54
rit.

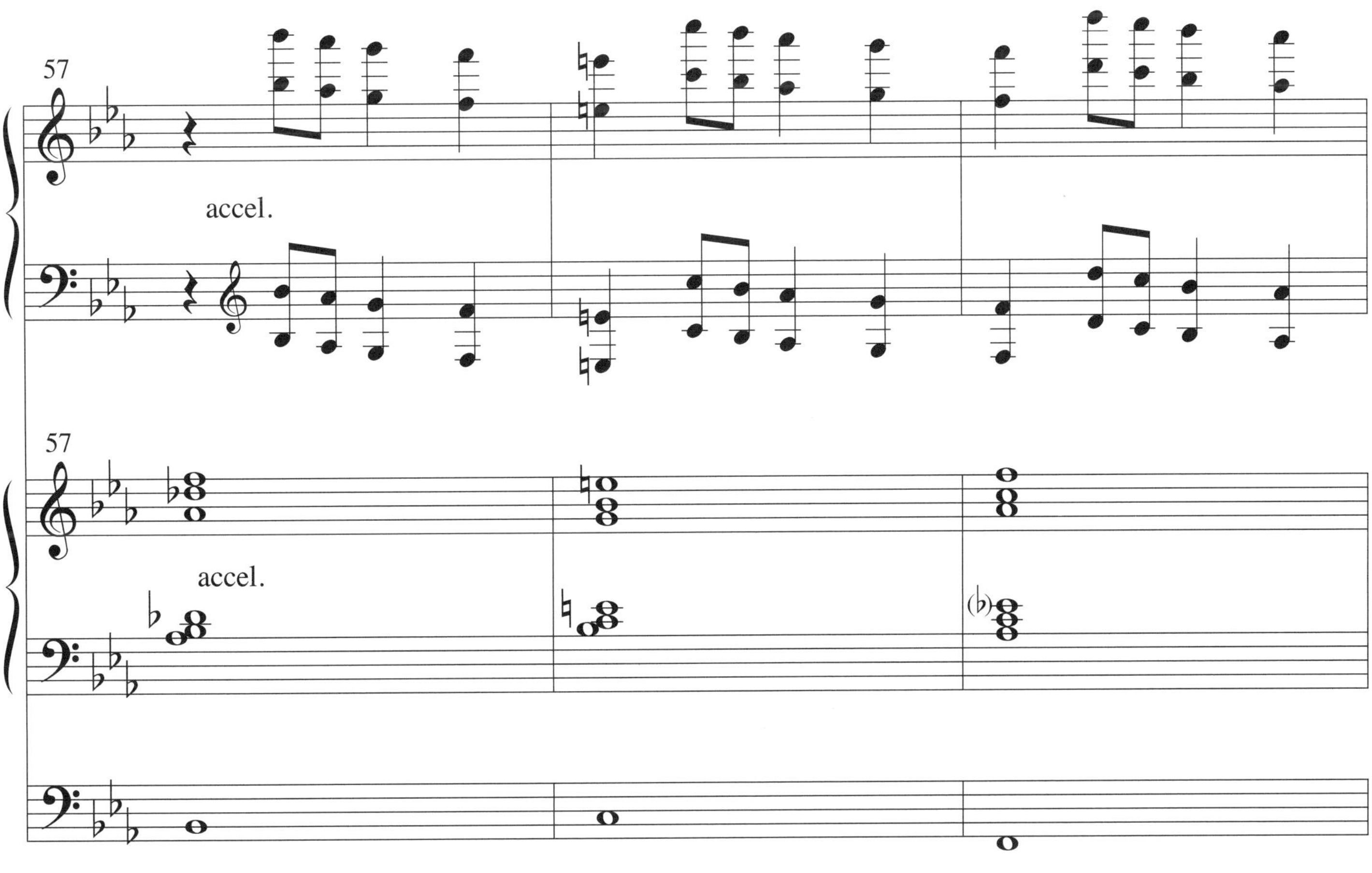
57
accel.
57
accel.

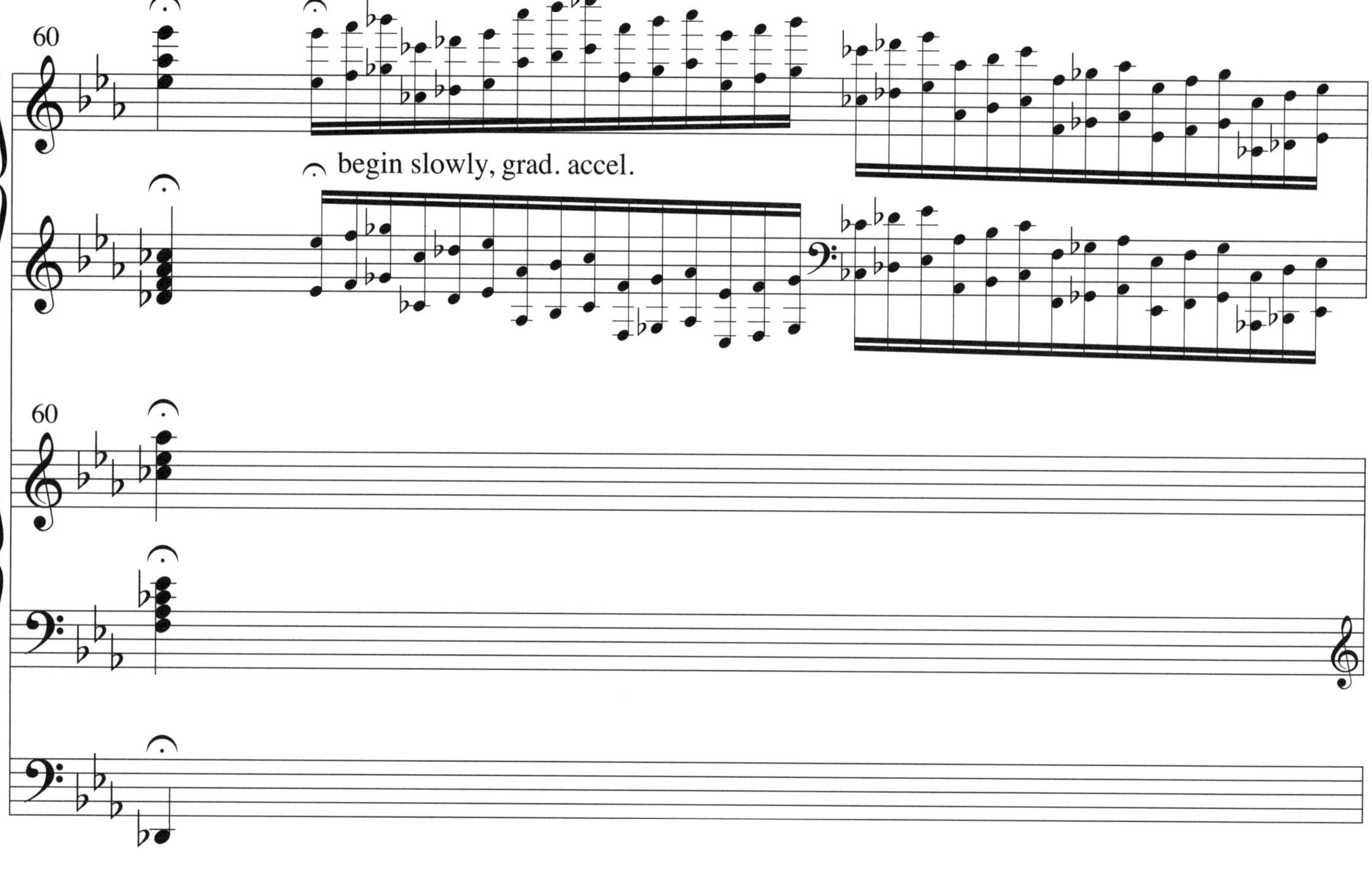
60
8va
begin slowly, grad. accel.
60

61
ff accel. poco a poco
61
ff accel. poco a poco

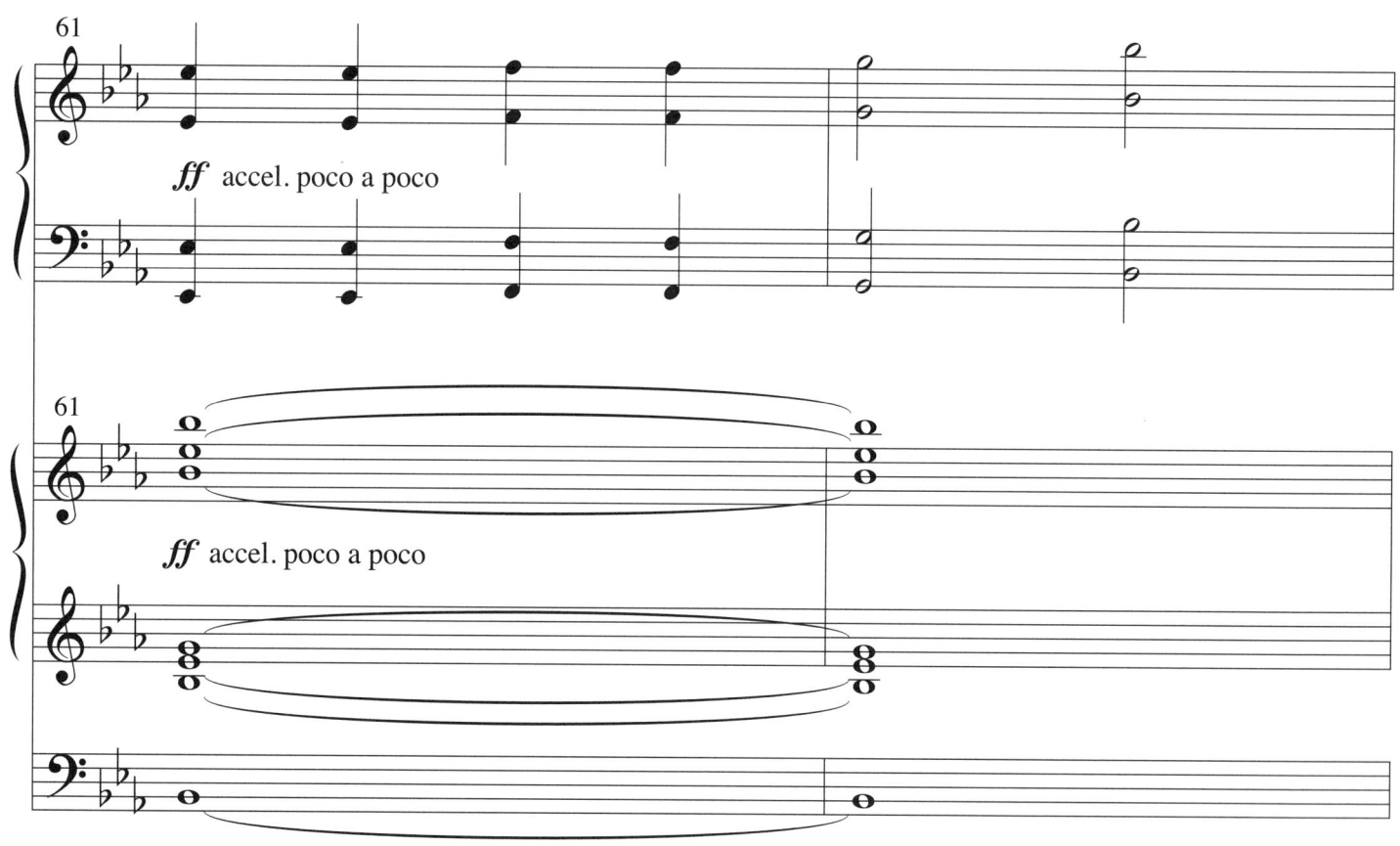

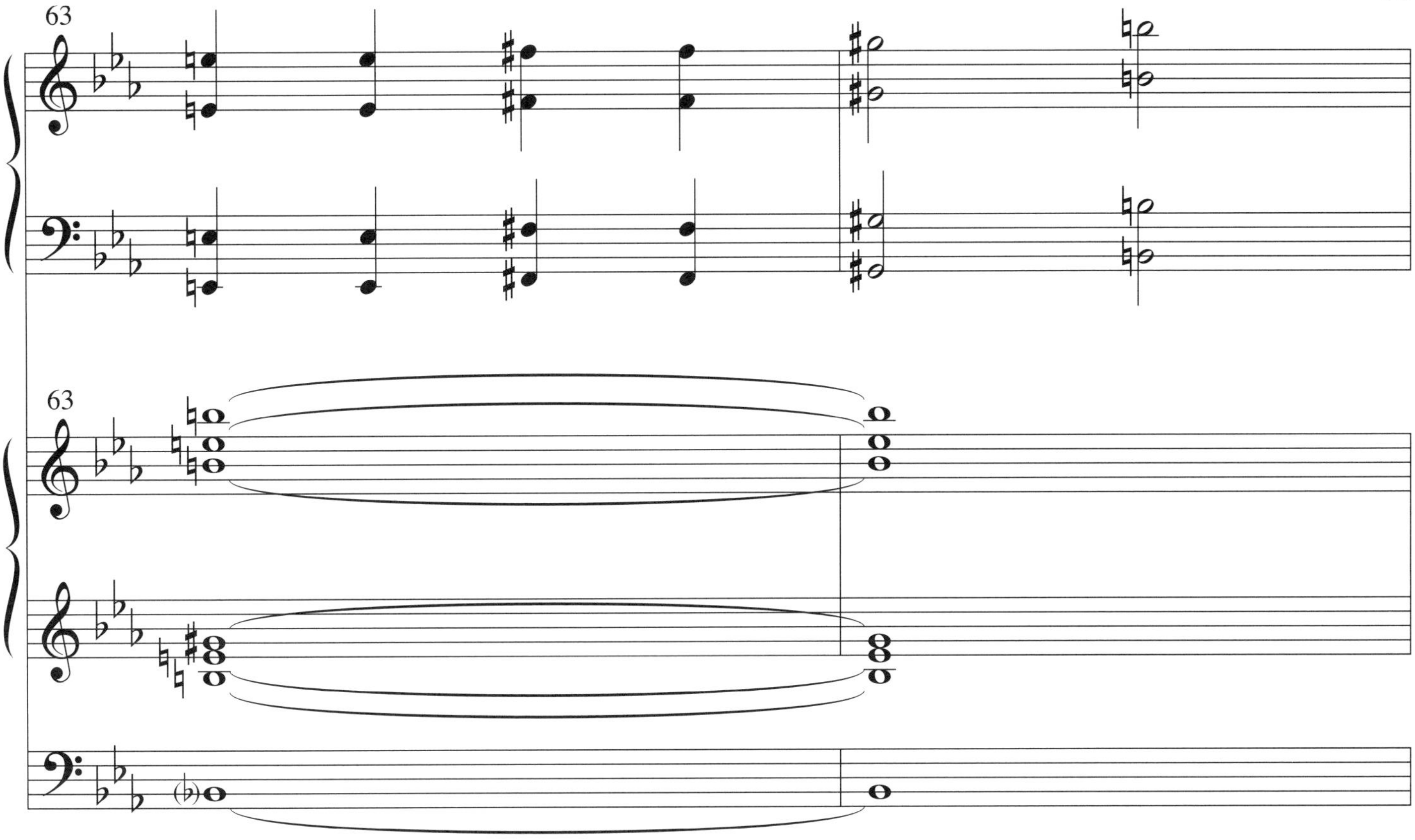
63
63

65
decresc.
65
decresc.

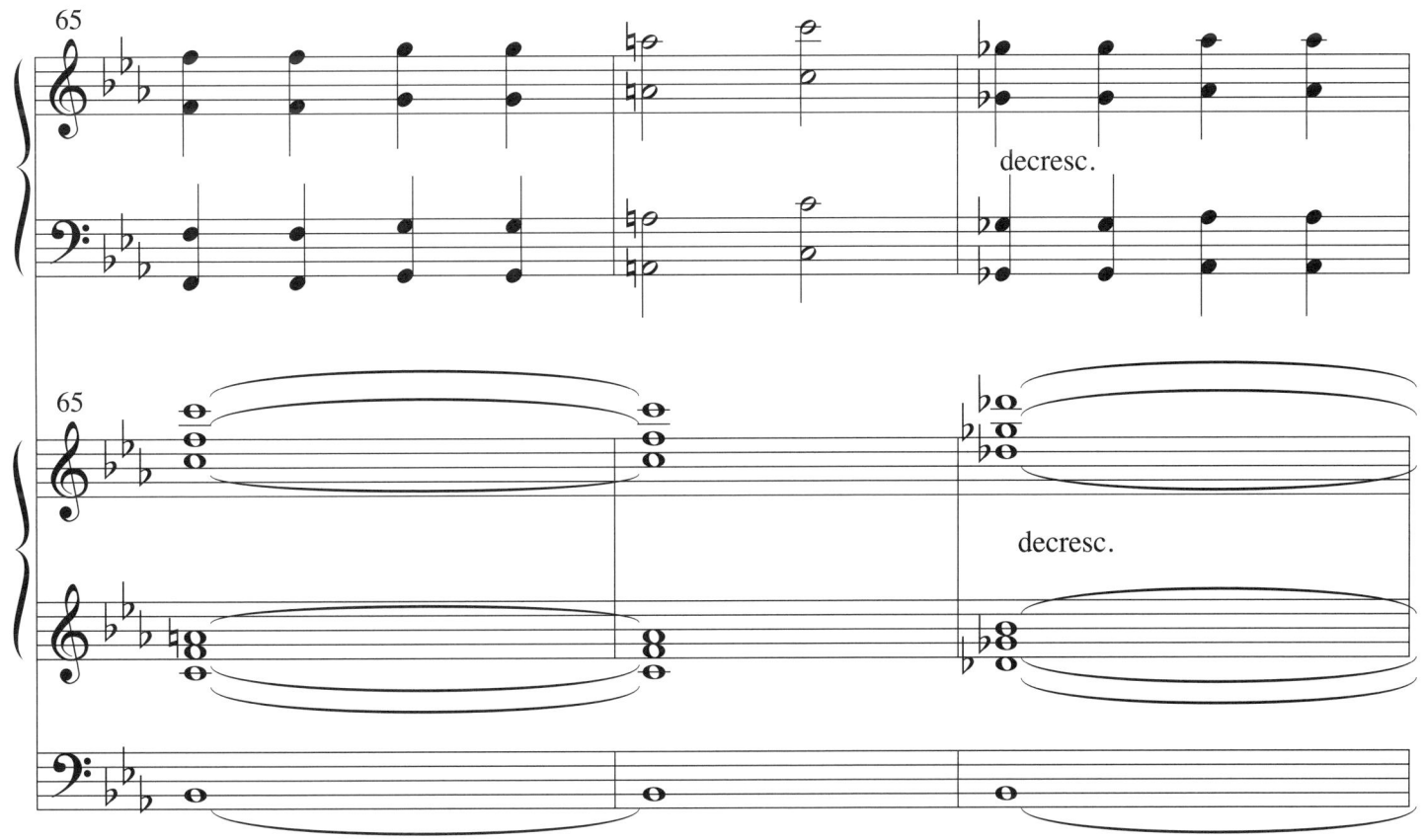

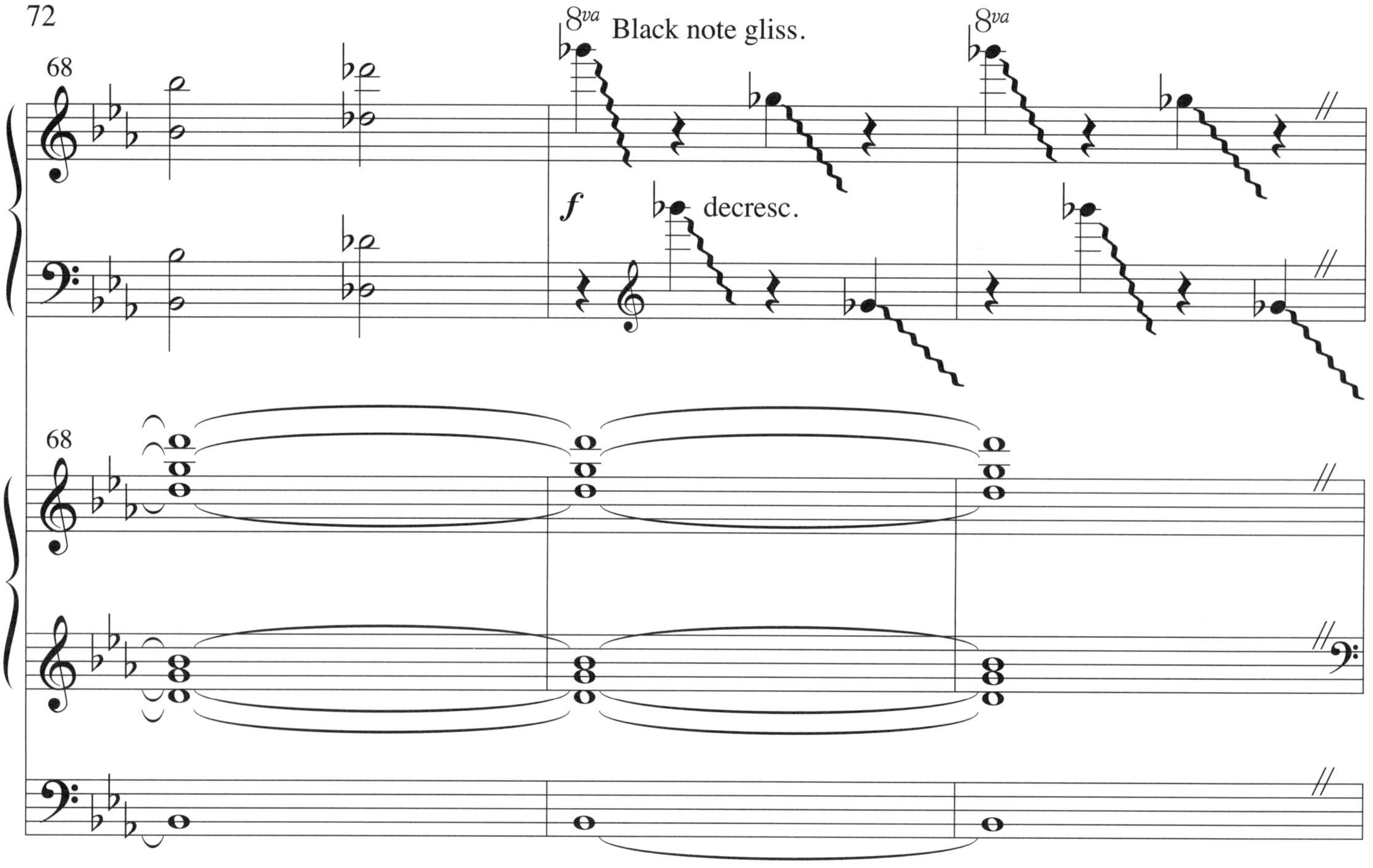
68
Black note gliss.
decresc.
68

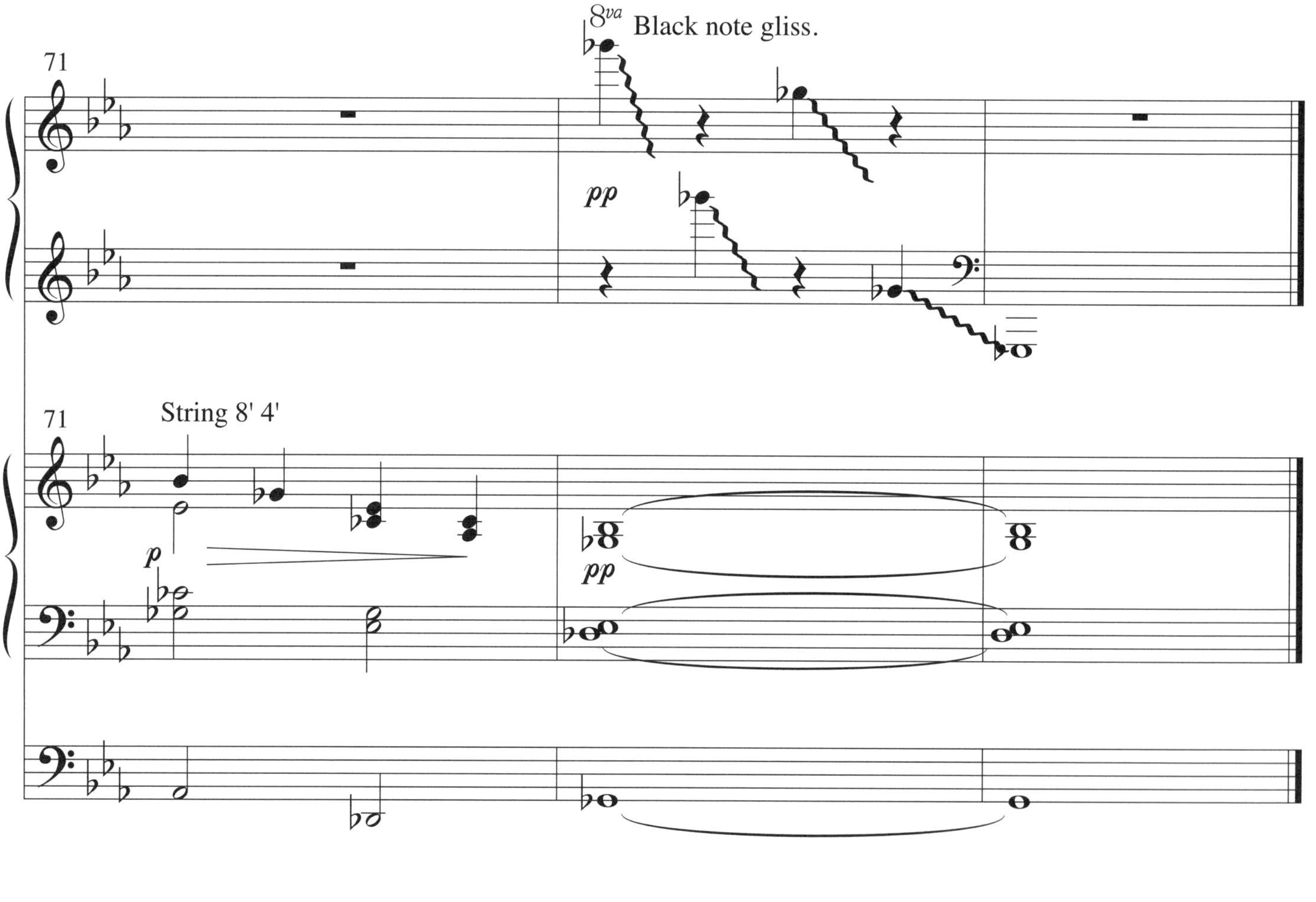
71
Black note gliss.
71
String 8' 4'

How Great Our Joy!

with
Angels, from the Realms of Glory

Sw. Principal 8', Octave 4', Flute 2'
Gt. Gedeckt 8', Lifflute 1'
Ped. Principal 16', Octave 8'

Traditional German Melody
Arranged by Paul Ferrin

Brightly ♩ = ca. 96

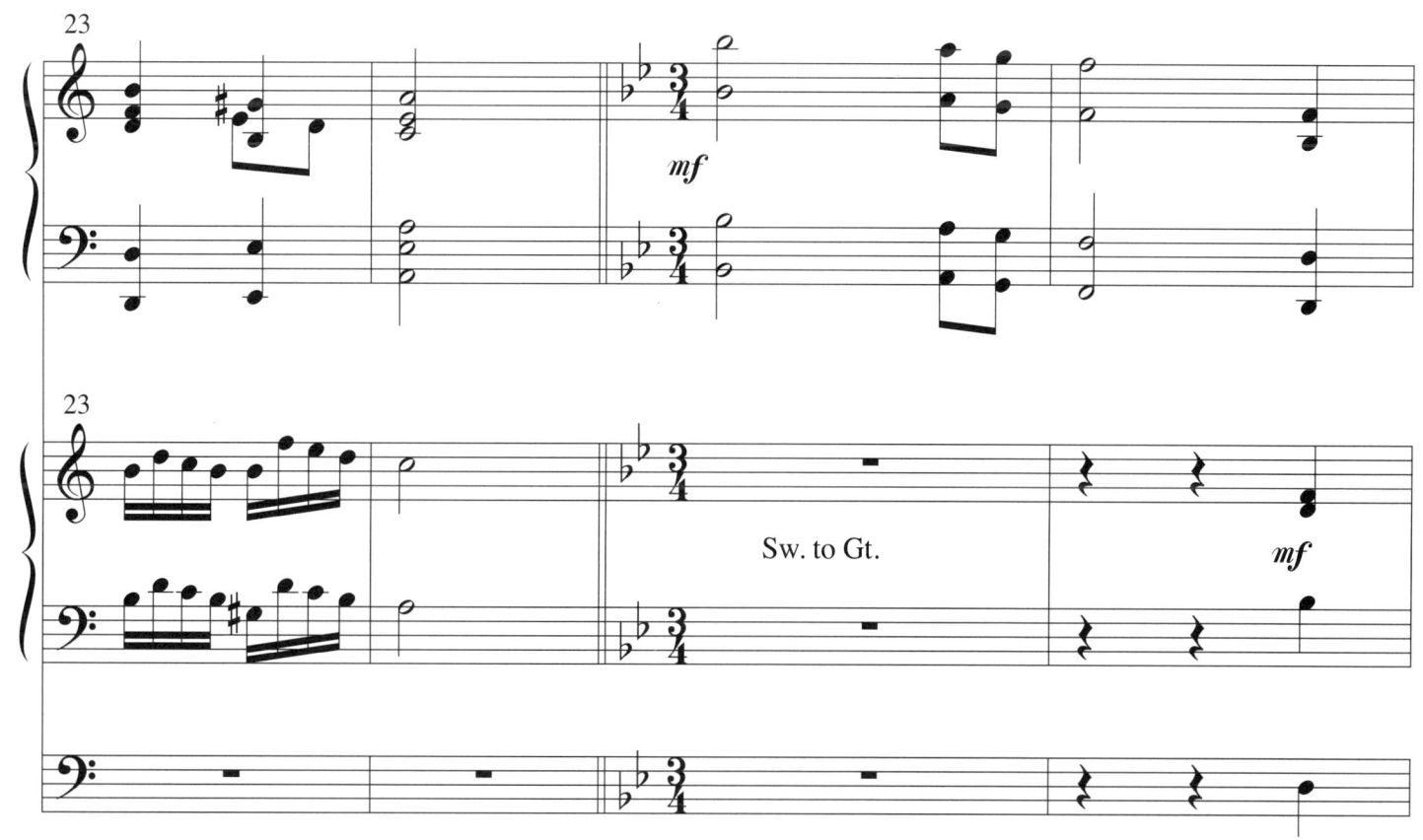

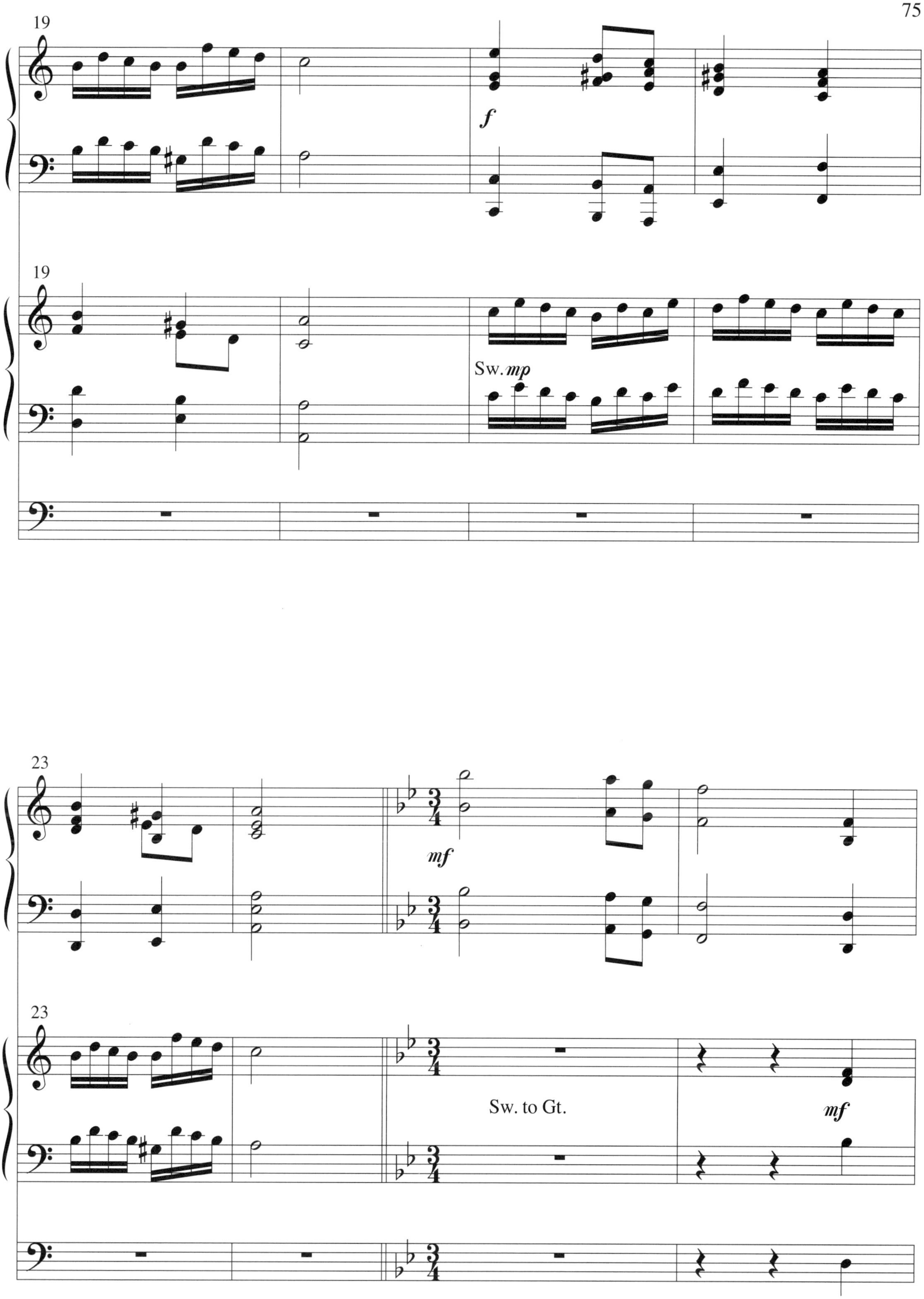
19
f
19
Sw. mp
23
mf
23
Sw. to Gt.
mf

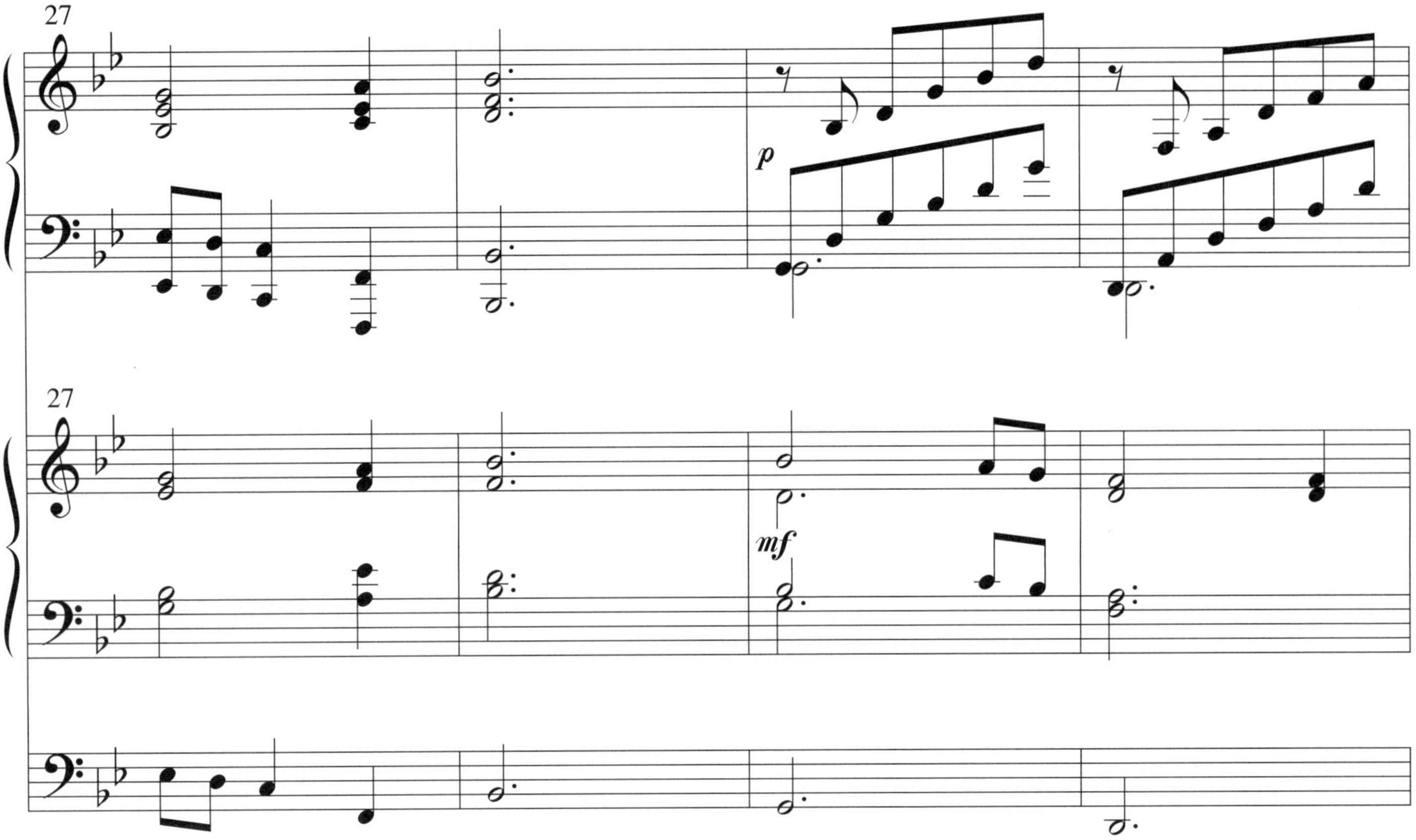
27
p
27
mf

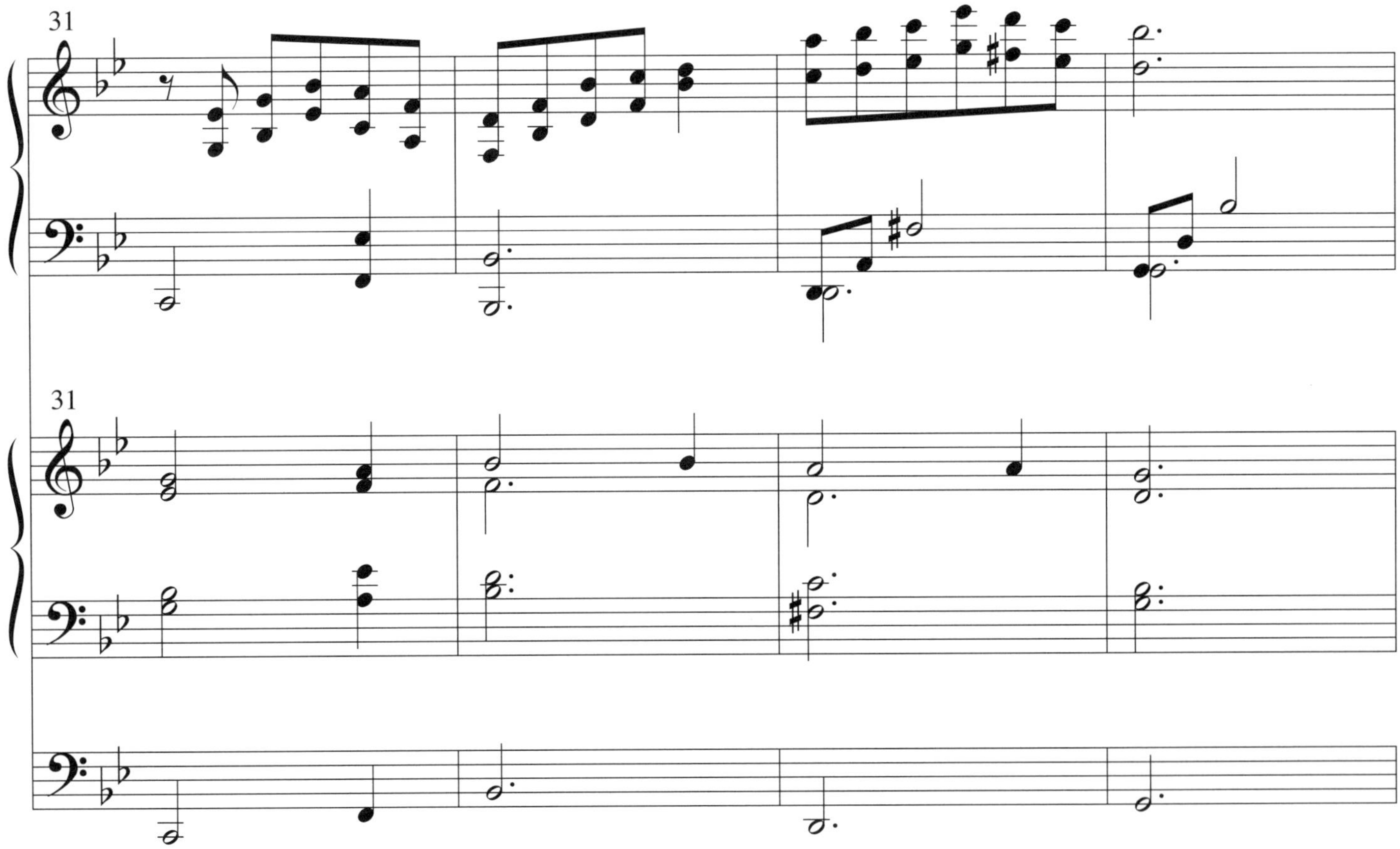
31
31

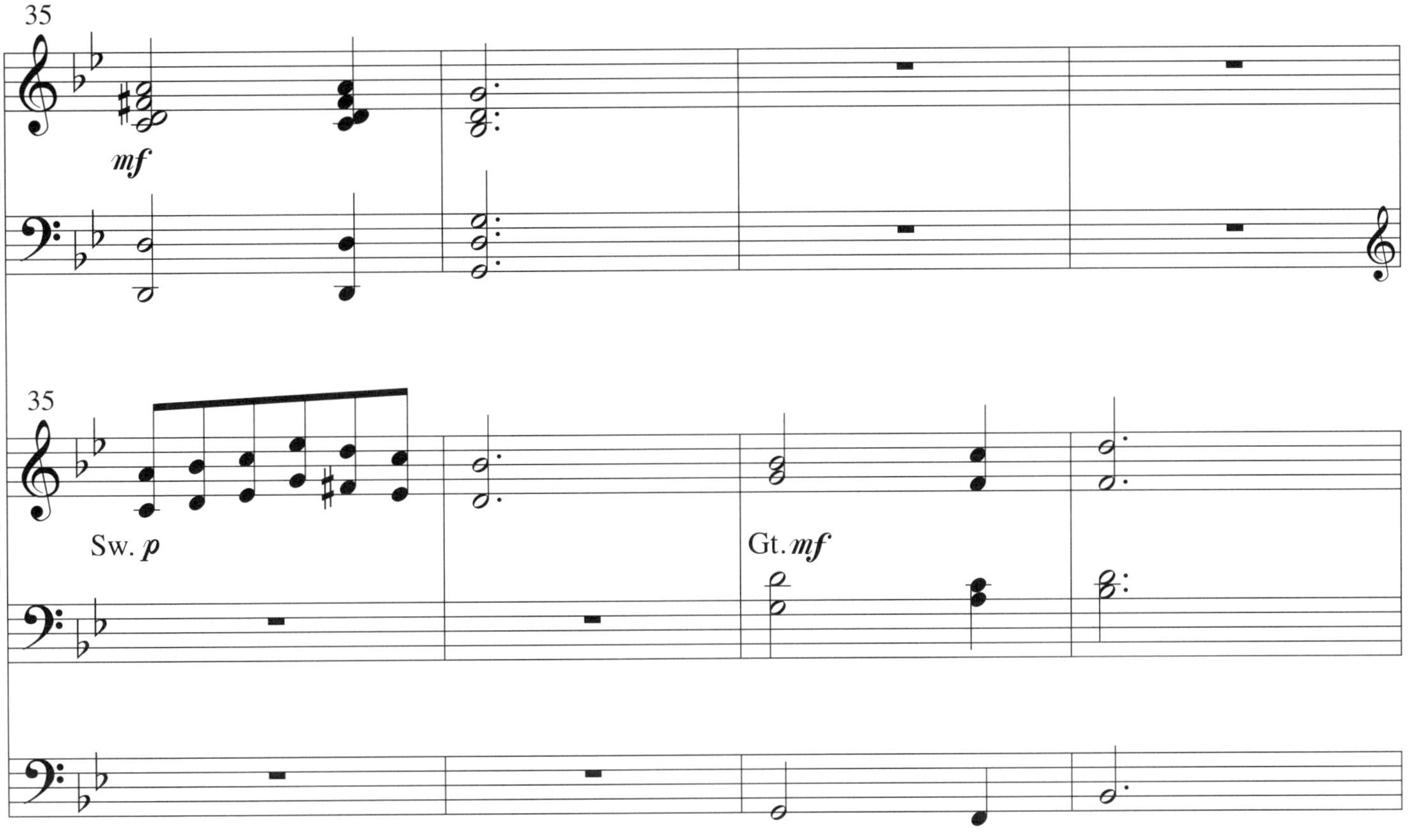
35
mf
35
Sw. p
Gt. mf

39
p
39
mf

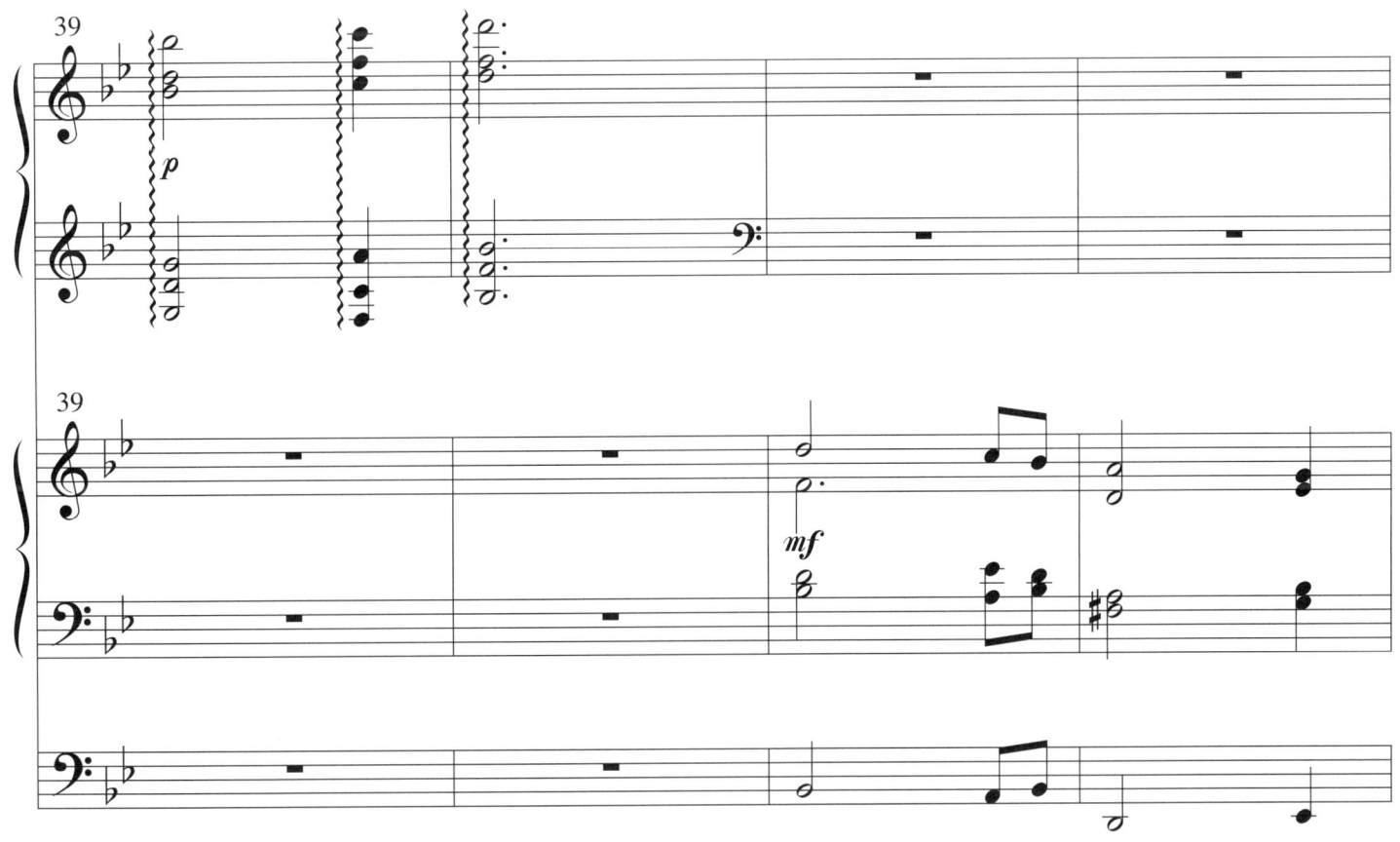

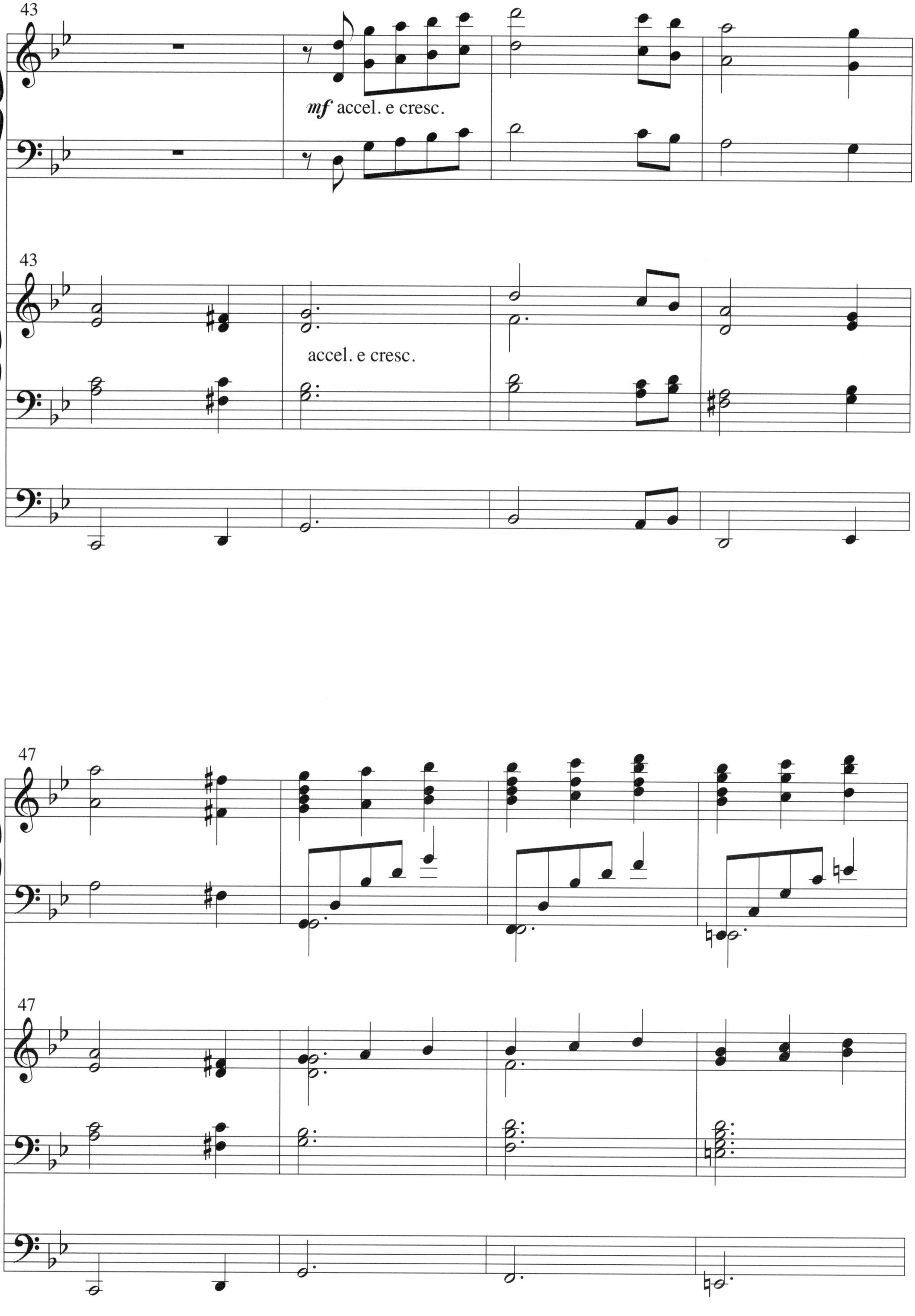
43
mf accel. e cresc.
43
accel. e cresc.
47
47

"Angels, from the Realms of Glory" (HENRY T. SMART)

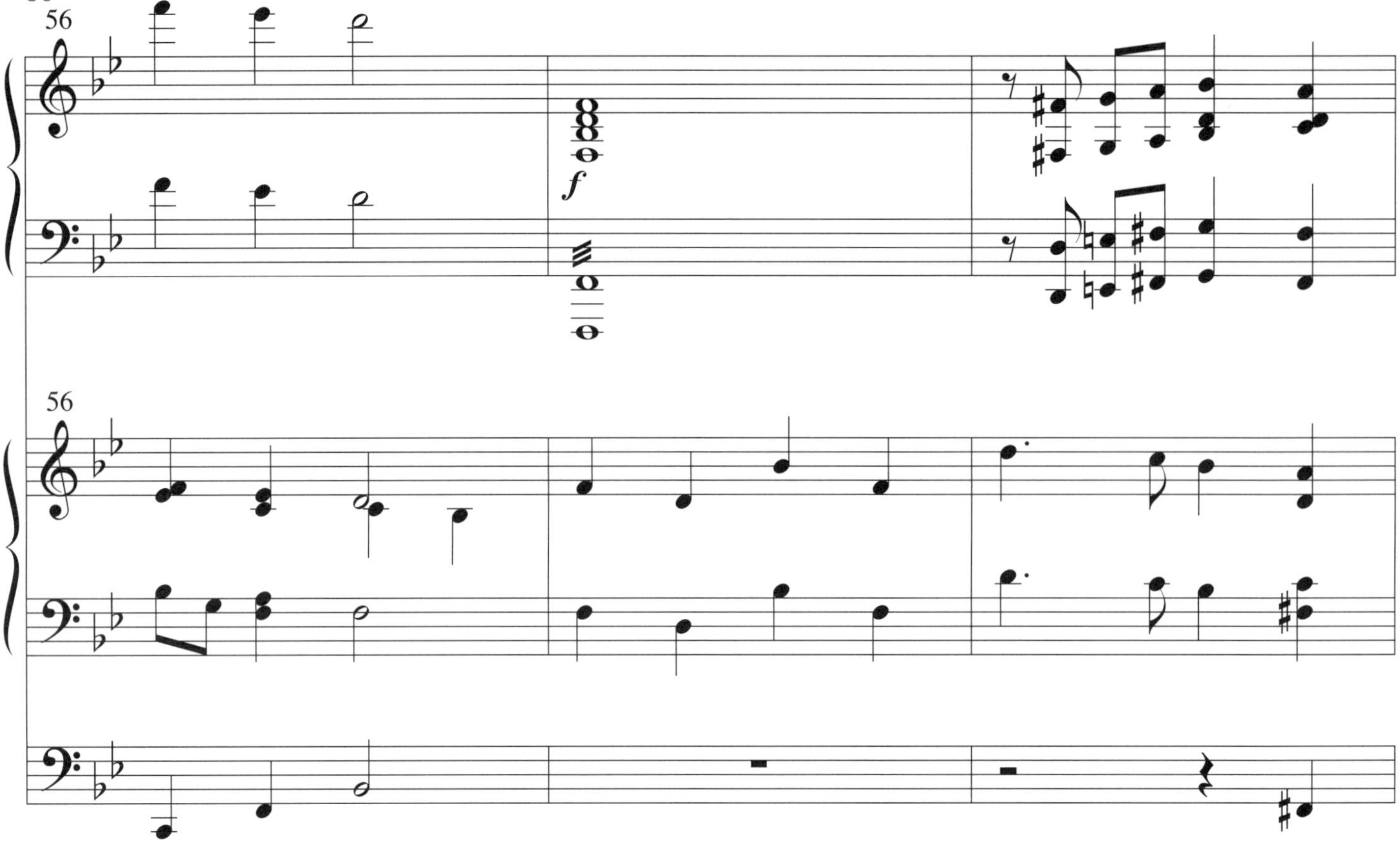
56
f
56

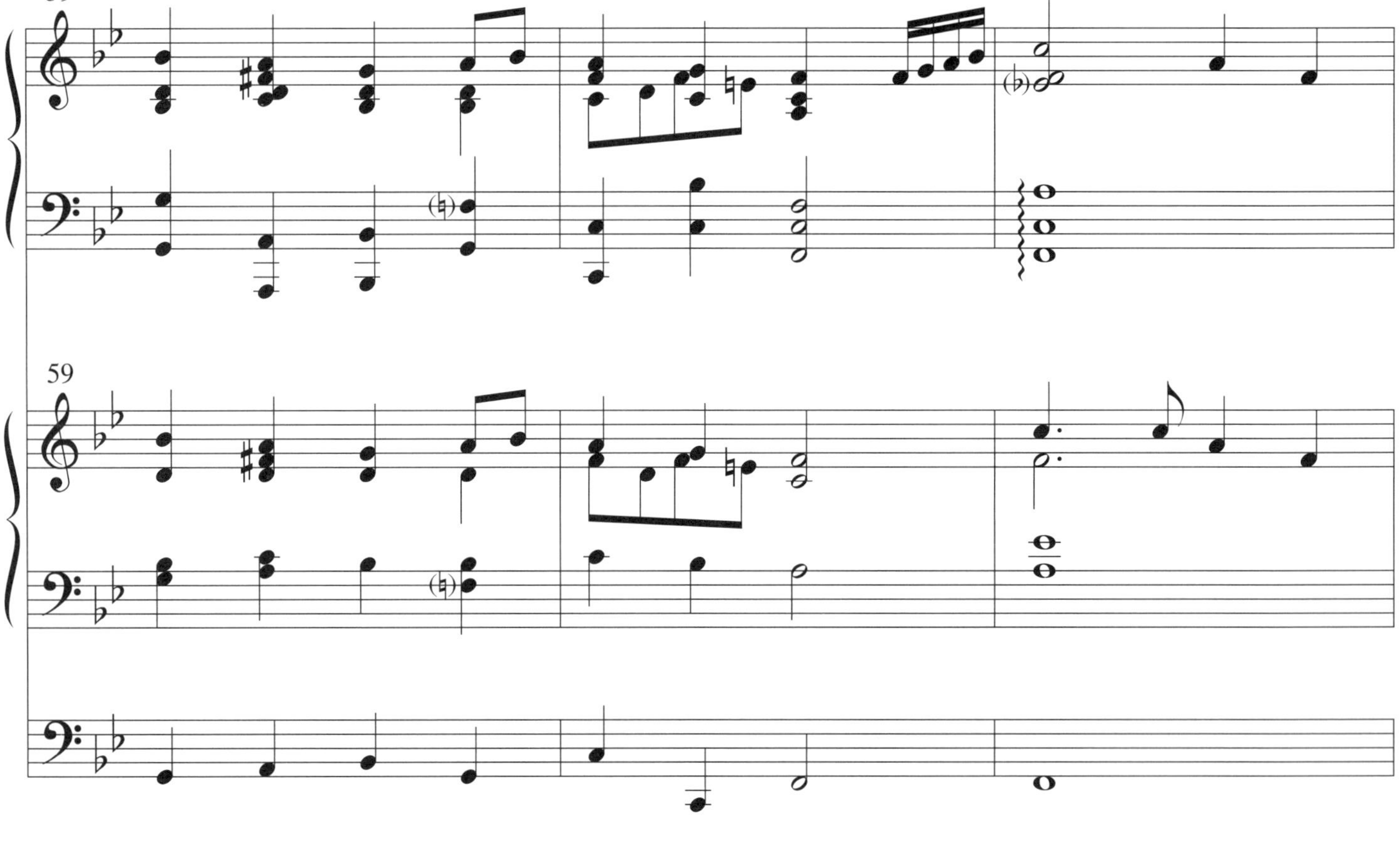
59
59

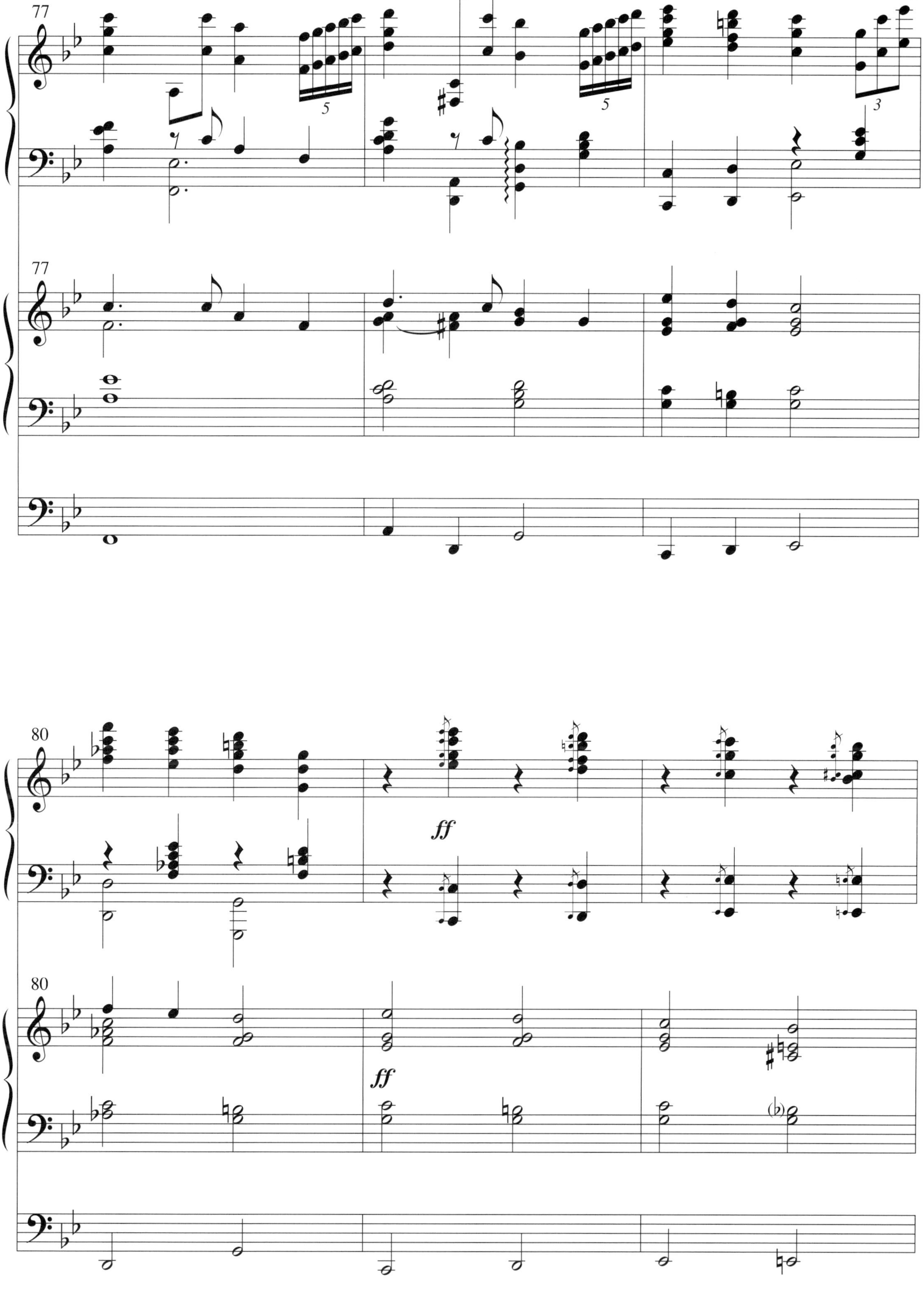
77
77
80
ff
80
ff

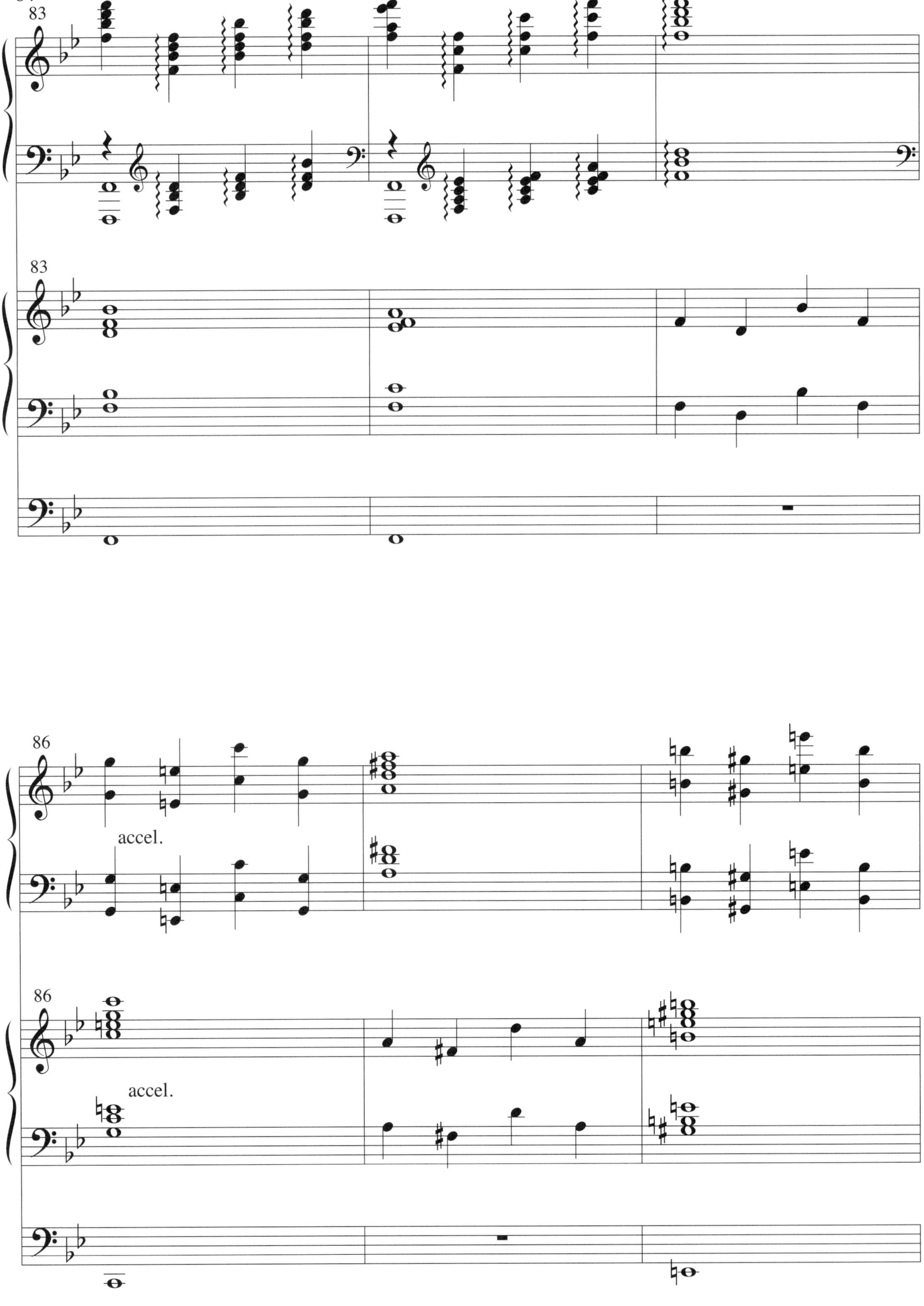
83
83
86
accel.
86
accel.

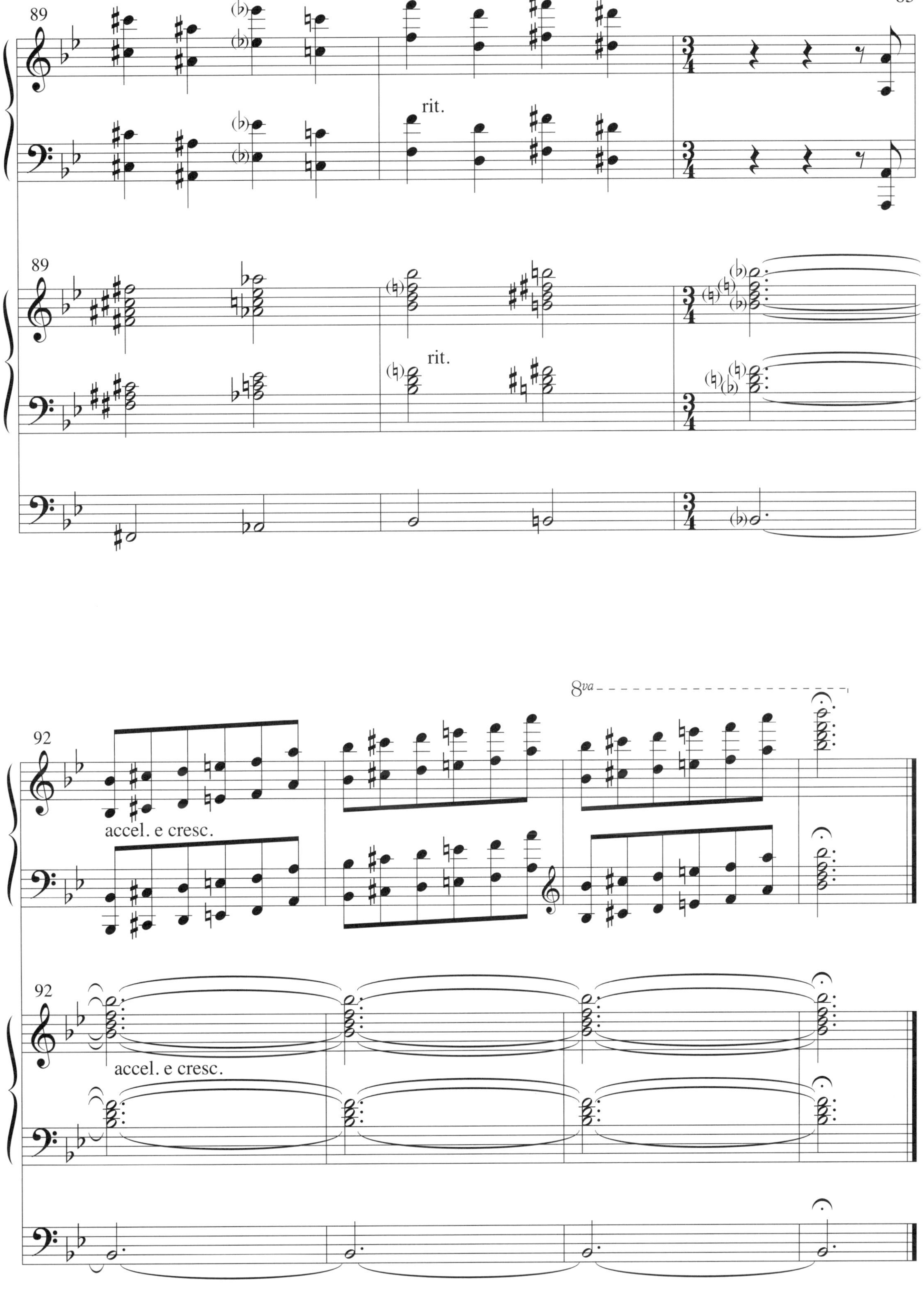
89
rit.
89
rit.
8va
92
accel. e cresc.
92
accel. e cresc.

O the Deep, Deep Love of Jesus

Sw. Gedeckt
Gt.   Krummhorn
Ped. Bourdon 16', Octave 8'

THOMAS J. WILLIAMS
Arranged by Paul Ferrin

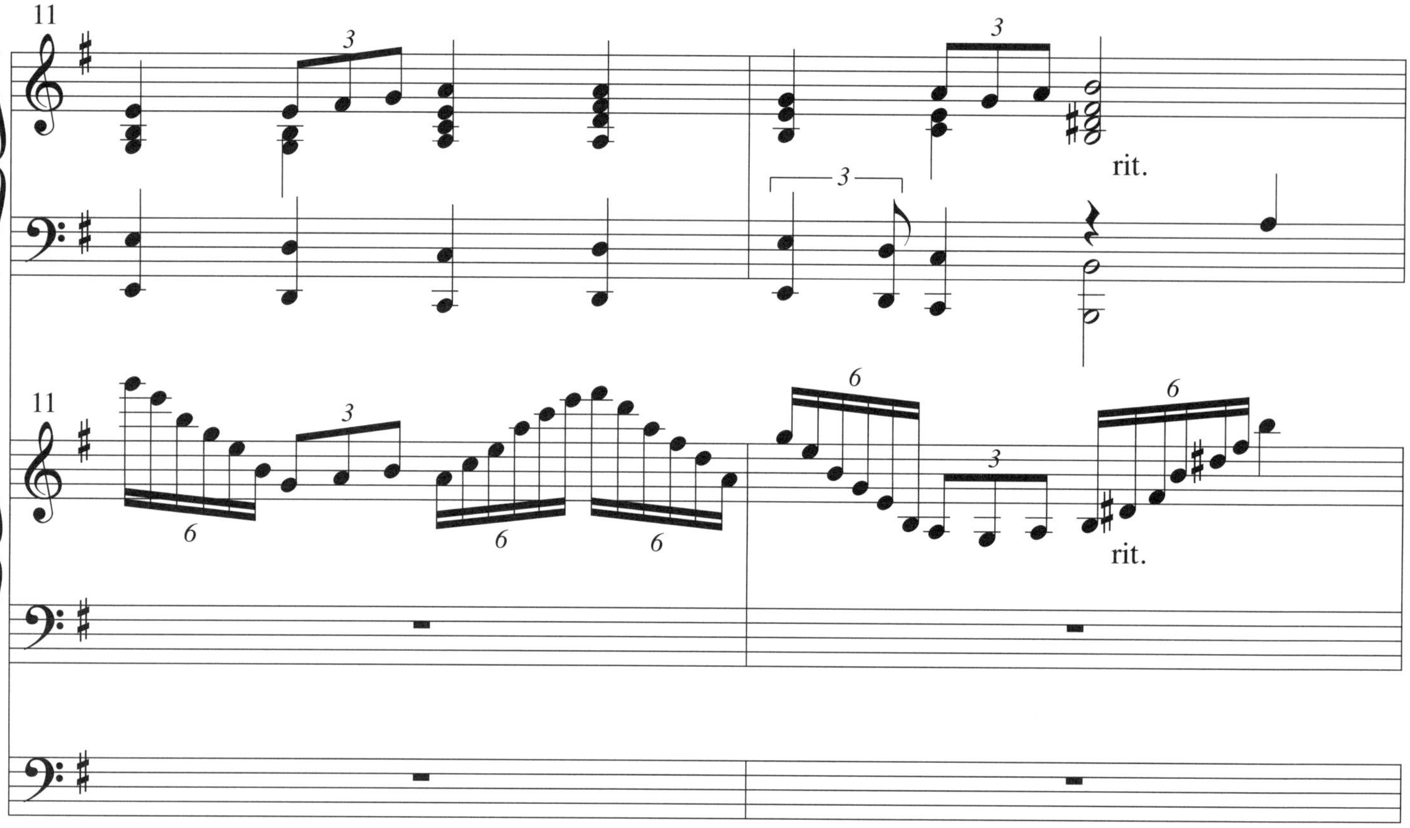
11
rit.
11
rit.

13
a tempo
p
13
Gt.
p a tempo

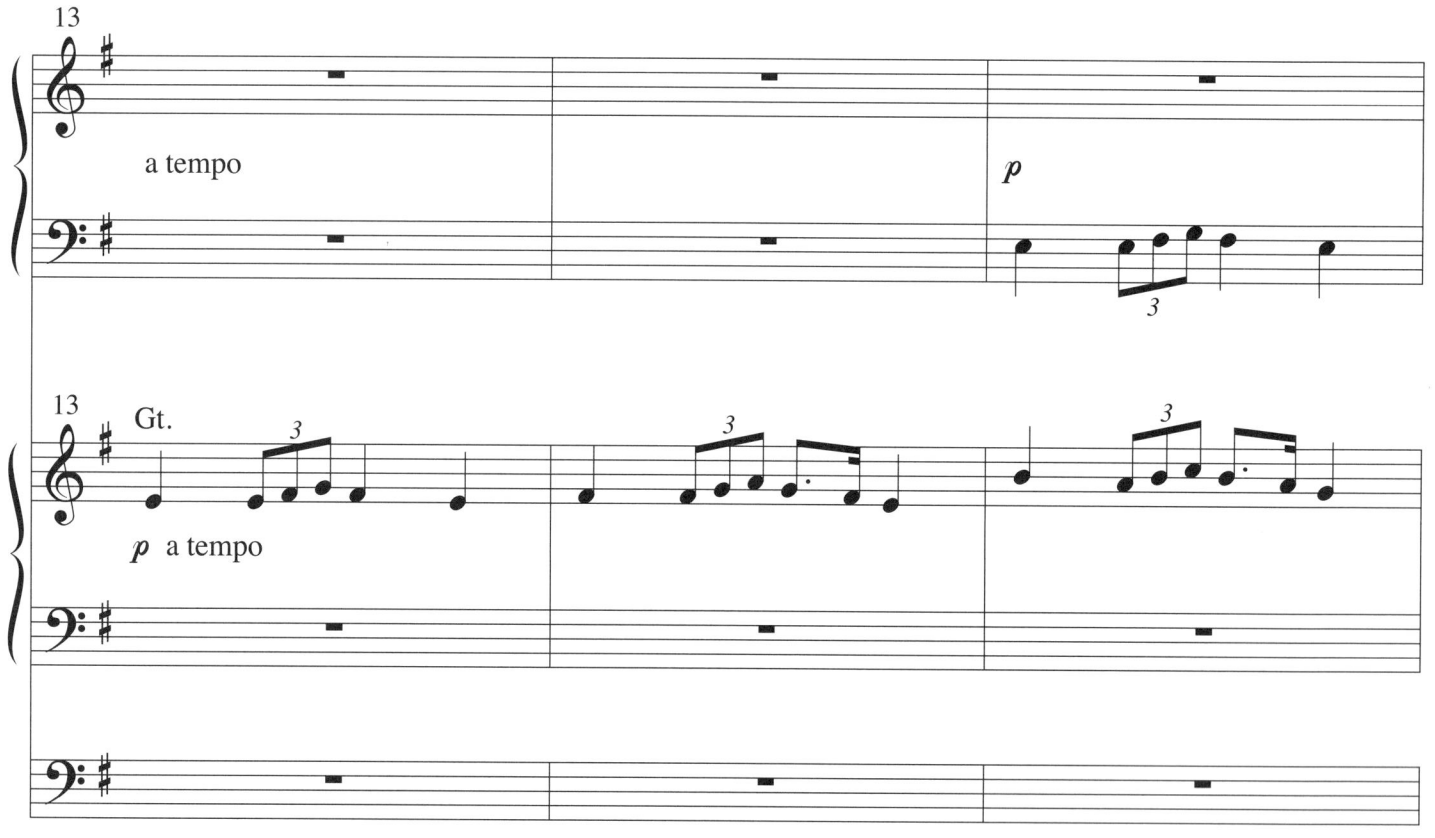

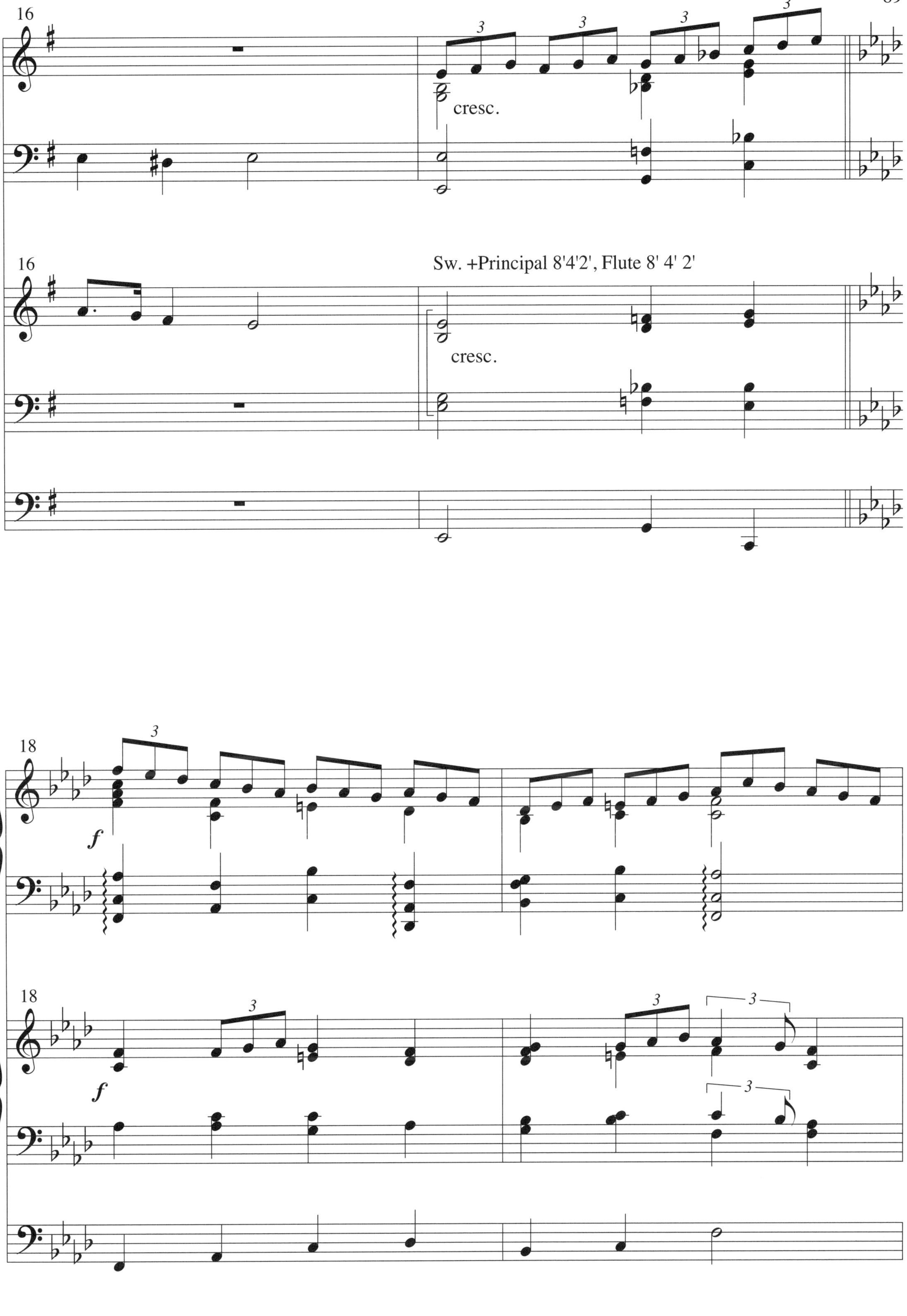
16
cresc.
16
Sw. +Principal 8'4'2', Flute 8' 4' 2'
cresc.
18
f
18
f

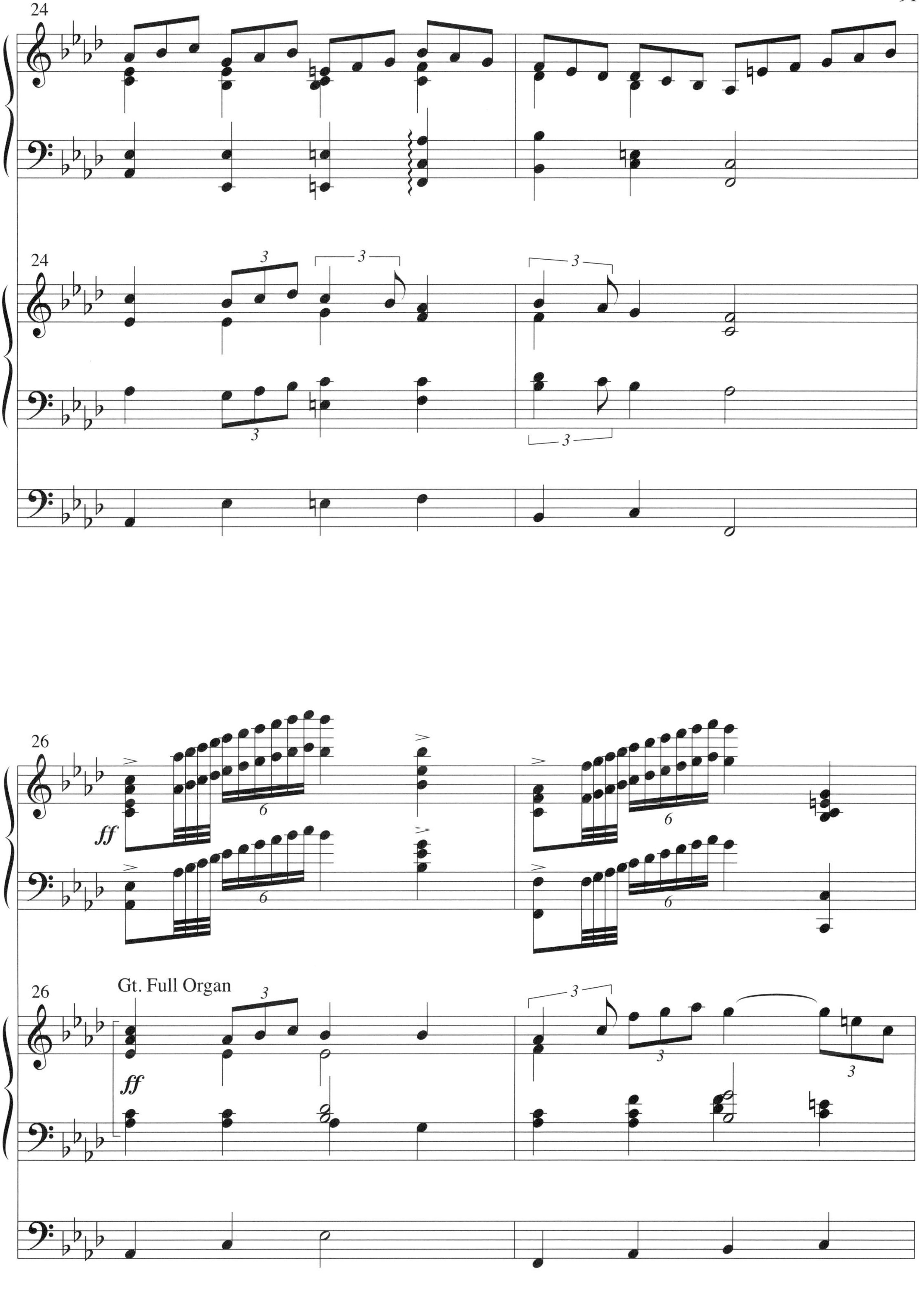
Gt. Full Organ

28
6
6
6
6
rit.
28
3
3
rit.
3
30
a tempo
30
Gt. Krummhorn
3
3
p a tempo

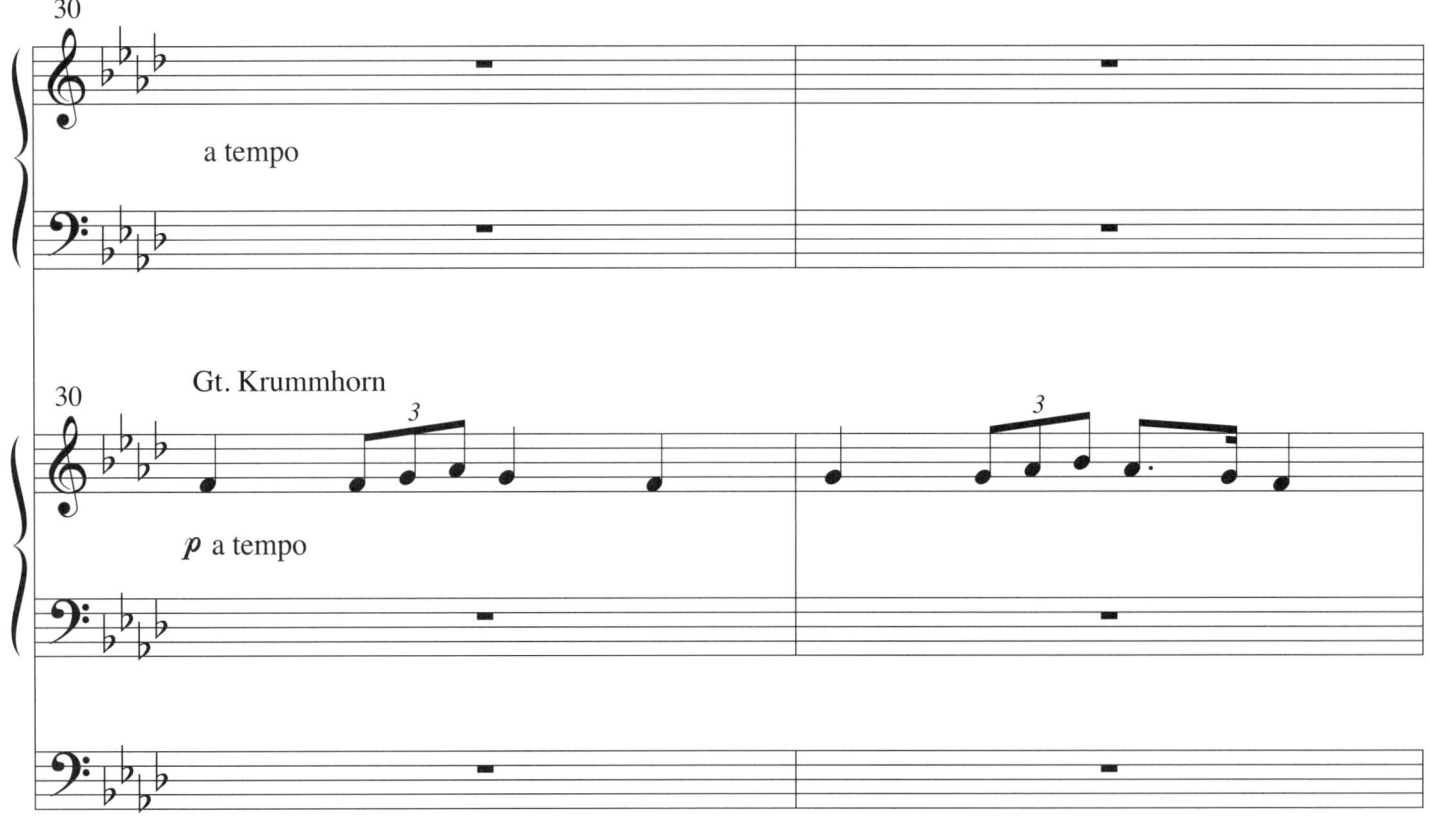

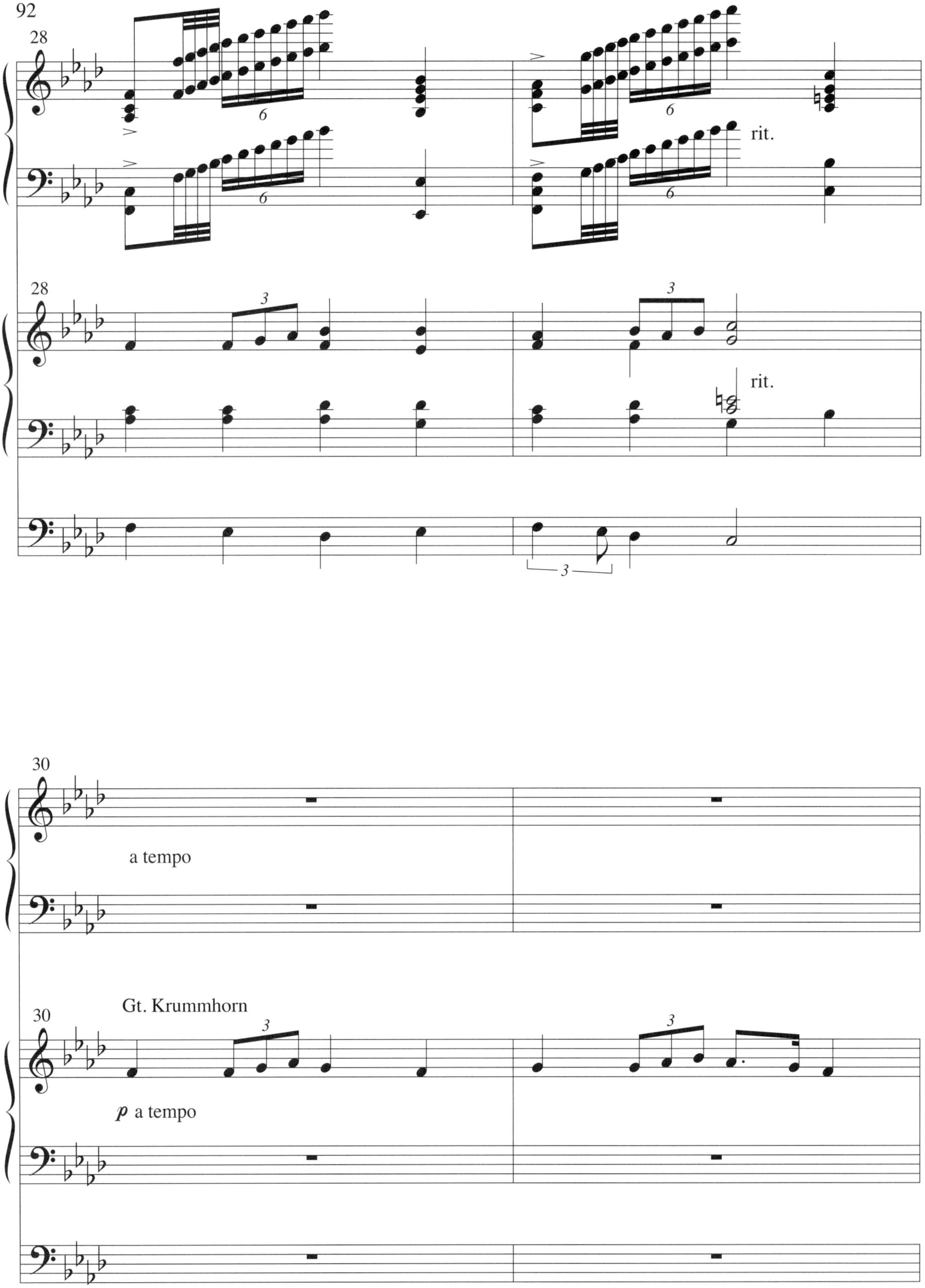

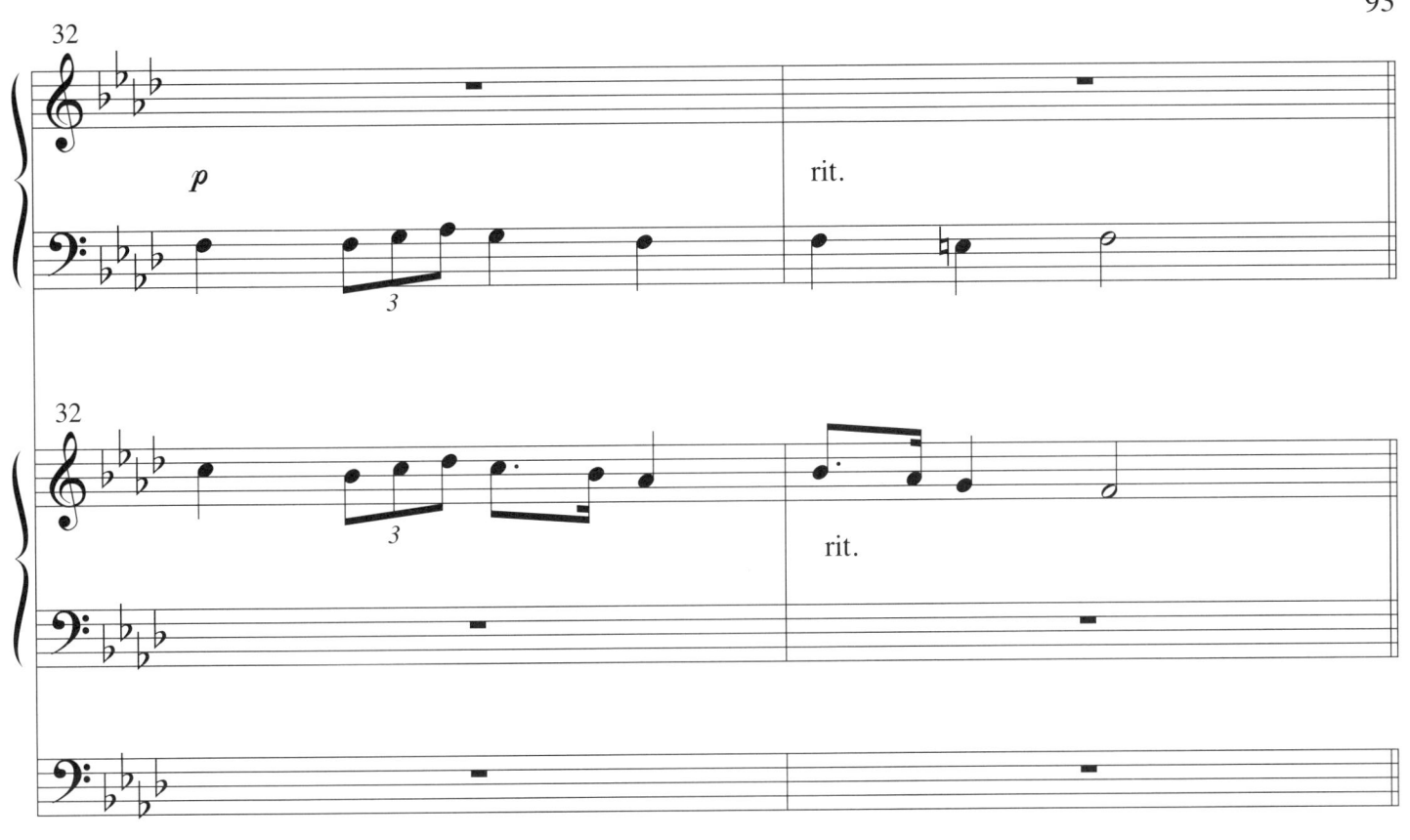

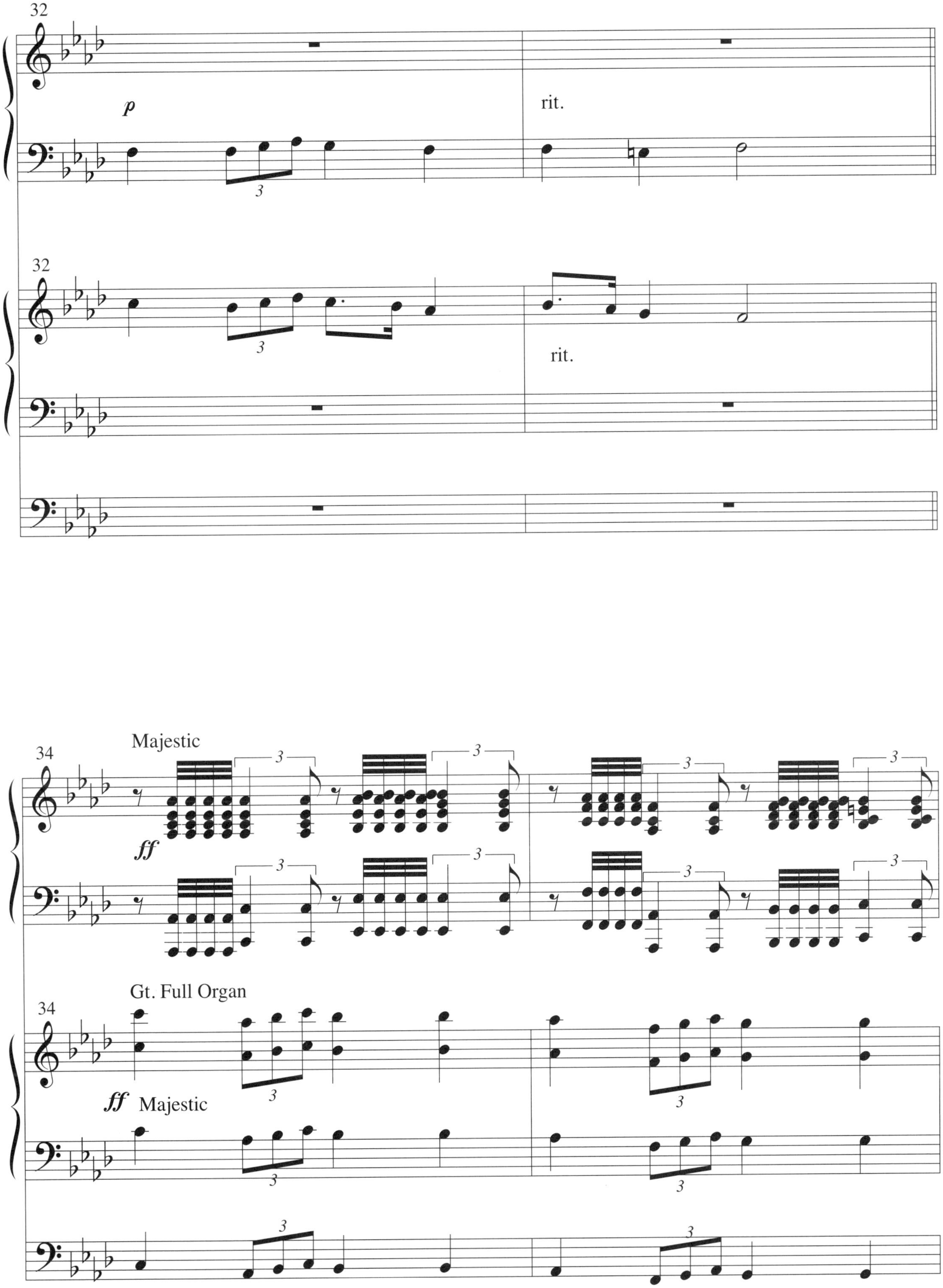
32
p
rit.
32
rit.
34
Majestic
ff
34
Gt. Full Organ
ff Majestic

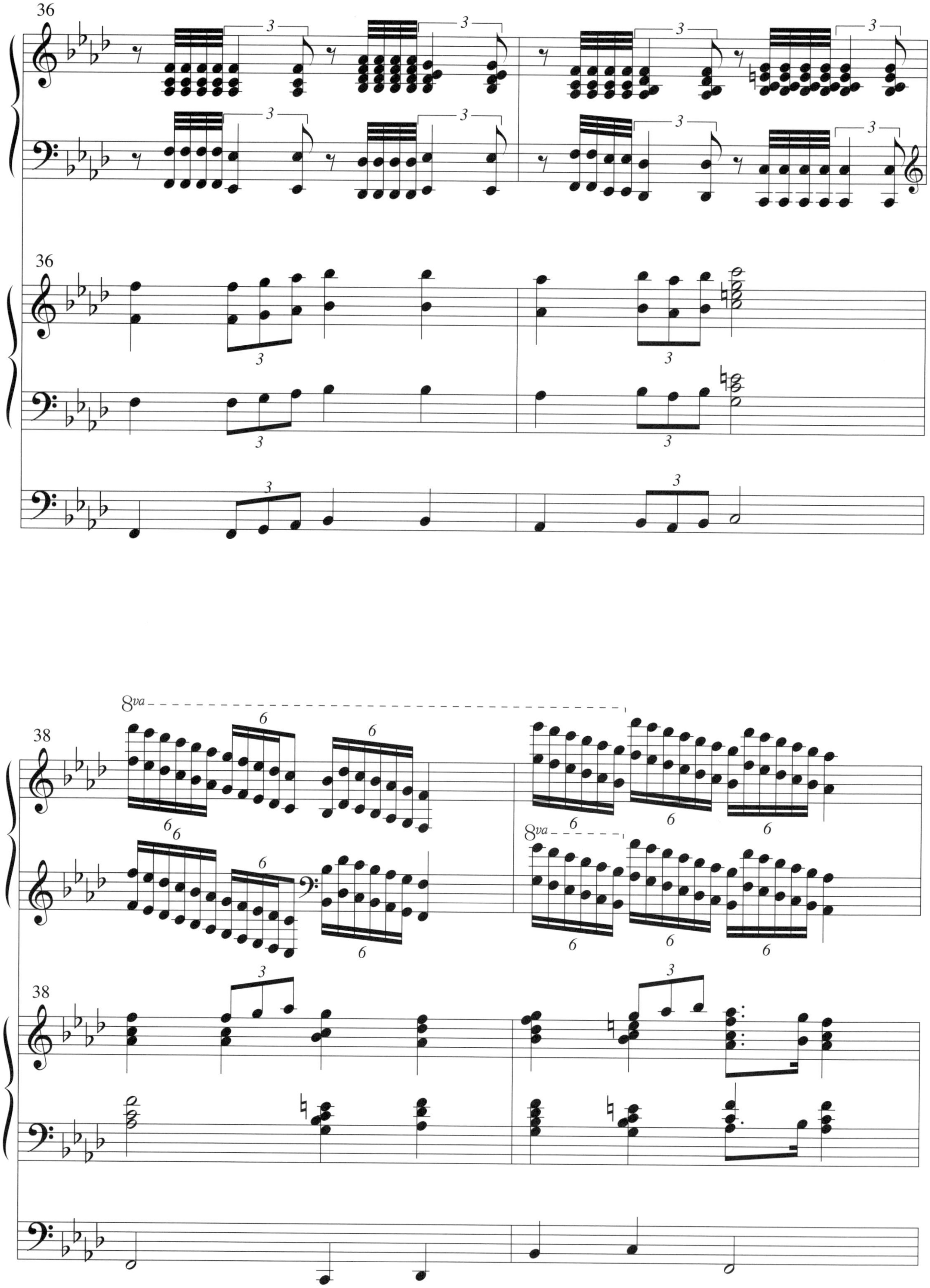
36
38
8va

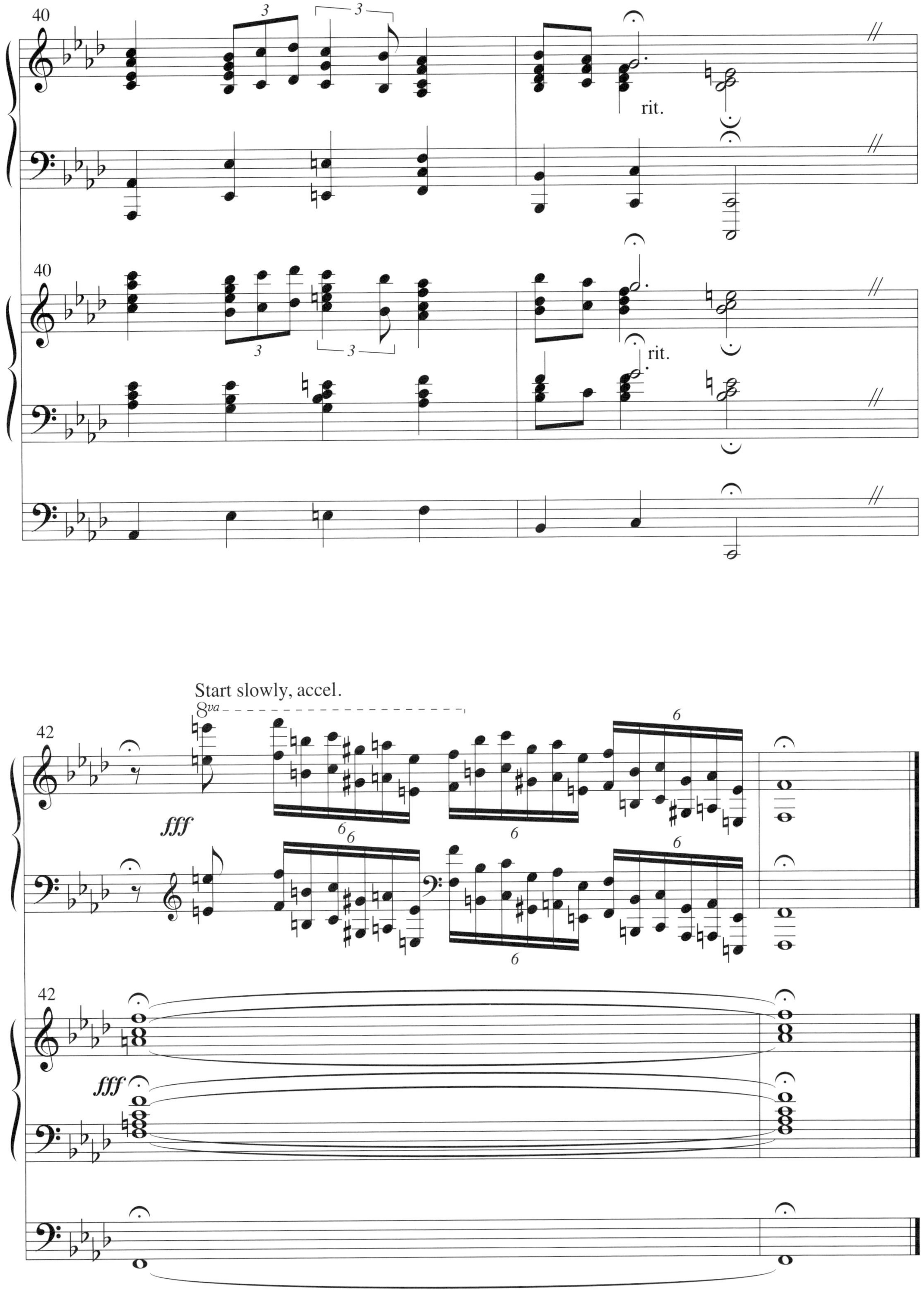
40
3
rit.
42
Start slowly, accel.
8va
fff
6